ABOUT THE AUTHOR

David Stafford is Director of St Joseph's Centre for Addiction in Haslemere, Surrey, and has a private practice in psychotherapy in Haslemere and London. He supervises the work of the Drug and Alcohol Rehabilitation Clinic, Guildford, an NHS facility, for South West Surrey Health Authority. He is a psychology graduate of Brunel University and is a fully trained psychoanalytic psychotherapist. His background includes voluntary work with down and outs with the Simon Community, intensive crisis intervention work with the Arbours Association in North London and residential social work in several therapeutic communities for the Richmond Fellowship including their specialist drug unit. David has carried out research in Social Services and Education and his first publication as a joint author was an academic book, *An Agreed Understanding*, NFER Nelson, 1987. It looks at parent – professional communication in relation to children with special educational needs.

David co-authored *Codependency* (Piatkus, 1991) with Liz Hodgkinson. With the use of case histories, this book shows how codependency starts, how it manifests itself and how the problems it causes can be overcome.

CHILDREN OF ALCOHOLICS

CHILDREN OF ALCOHOLICS

How a parent's drinking
can affect your life

DAVID STAFFORD

PIATKUS

First published in 1992 by
Judy Piatkus (Publishers) Ltd of
5 Windmill Street, London W1P 1HF

The moral right of the author has been asserted

*A catalogue record for this book is available
from the British Library*

ISBN 0 – 7499 – 1140 – 9

Cover design by Jennie Smith
Edited by Maggie Daykin

Set in Compugraphic Baskerville 11 ½ pt by
Action Typesetting Limited, Gloucester
Printed and bound in Great Britain by
Billing and Sons Ltd, Worcester

To my children Lucy, Jamie, and Katy, and to the memory of Marie Therese Haze, founder of the Congregation of the Daughters of the Cross, beatified in Rome in 1991. Marie Therese knew well the pain of early loss. She lived in the aftermath of the French revolution and transformed her own experience of personal tragedy into a tremendous example of faith in action. Her life and works have inspired many to acts of courage and kindness.

ACKNOWLEDGEMENTS

I would like to thank Chris Hinton, Sister Mary Agnes, Dr Tony Baker, and the congregation of the Daughters of the Cross for their support and encouragement to me in writing this book. I am grateful too for the help of my wife Sue as the book began to take shape. She read each page in first draft and made helpful criticisms and suggestions. Appreciation is also due to Dr Diana Samways, Hilary Henriques, Val Magee, Maya Parker, Neil Kelly, Maria Kelly, Sue Stafford, and John Dane from the National Association for Children of Alcoholics. To the staff at St Joseph's Centre I extend warm thanks. I have learned a great deal from their work with addiction patients and their families, some of which is reflected in these pages. To Gill Cormode of Piatkus Books and Maggie Daykin, my editor, I shall always be thankful; they pulled no punches and the result is a book which is more reader friendly than otherwise would have been the case.

Finally, I would like to thank all those children of alcoholics who have spoken to me about their experiences. Especially I would like to thank Neil, Michael and Jenny, who not only consented to having their stories included in this book but expressed a deep-felt desire that others might find hope and encouragement in reading them.

Contents

ST JOSEPH'S CENTRE

St Joseph's Centre for Addiction, at the Holy Cross Hospital, Haslemere, was established in 1986 to offer a multi-disciplinary and holistic approach to the treatment of adults addicted to various substances, including alcohol and illicit drugs. The Centre, which has fourteen beds and outpatient facilities, is sited in self-contained premises in the grounds of the hospital. It enjoys charitable status through its association with the parent hospital which is run by the Congregation of the Daughters of the Cross, a respected contributor to charitable services in this and other countries.

The residential chemical dependency treatment programme at St Joseph's is of six weeks duration. The Centre uses two principal methods to achieve the aim of equipping people to live a drug free way of life – the Minnesota Method and Family Therapy. The Minnesota Method includes lectures, group therapy, and life skills training, and aims to teach a new way of life based on freedom from mind altering substances. It is St Joseph's policy to view addiction as a family illness and it offers considerable support and education to family members on an outpatient basis. Family Therapy can be essential to put changes into context for those families with other serious problems in addition to those of drugs and alcohol, and where the problems preclude a good recovery from addiction.

St Joseph's offers various services to children of alcoholics of all ages and other codependents on an outpatient basis through the Codependency Clinic. In addition to an assessment and referral service it also provides individual and group counselling, psychotherapy and family therapy.

St Joseph's, being a charity, welcomes donations to further its work.

Introduction:
Invisible People

IF YOU read this book with the knowledge that you are the grown-up child of an alcoholic and that your life has been affected in important ways by the drinking pattern of one, or both, parents, then I wish you well in your continued recovery. I hope that, as intended, this book will provide you with support, and offer new insights into the effects of parental drinking on your life. In fact, you are one of the lucky ones, as few children of alcoholics quite appreciate how their childhood experiences affected them, and continue to do so. You are a rare individual and quite uncommon in your knowledge.

The effects of parental drinking on children tend to be concealed by the children themselves, by their parents – including the non-drinking one – by schools, doctors, psychologists, and social workers. The 'concealment' is not a malicious or even conscious act; we just have not had the knowledge and understanding which is available today, or the will to face up to the problems parental drinking can cause. This book provides important facts about the family illness we call alcoholism, gives voice to the experiences of those who are coming to terms with their family legacy, and provides encouragement and guidance for anyone who has grown up in the shadow of an alcoholic parent. If this has been your experience, be assured that you are by no means alone – and you can be helped. Let reading this book be the first step on your pathway to a happy and fulfilling life.

'The invisible population'

The number of children of alcoholics is estimated to be in the range of one to five million people in the UK alone, depending on the definition of alcoholism used. In Chapter 1, I consider in more detail just how the scale of the problem might be estimated. But however the figure is arrived at, it is quite remarkable how such a large number of affected individuals could have remained unidentified for so long – and it is why children of alcoholics have been called 'the invisible population'. They have remained so for many reasons.

The stigma of alcoholism

The single greatest hurdle to bringing the effects of alcoholism into the open is the stigma attached to it in our society. We continue to isolate and castigate the alcoholic for his lack of self-control and blame him for exhibiting the symptoms of what we now know to be an identifiable and treatable illness. We do not blame the diabetic for his failure to produce insulin in sufficient quantities, nor do we refuse him treatment until he does so. Yet, with alcoholics, we use a prime symptom of the illness (loss of control), as evidence of his untreatability. We reinforce the very way that the illness perpetuates itself by blaming the alcoholic for his apparent 'weakness of character'.

Such negative behaviour hardly facilitates the alcoholic seeking help but rather encourages him to remain in hiding, and to keep his children in hiding. As we shall see in Chapter 3, the illness thrives on shame and secretiveness, which makes the stigma doubly inappropriate.

We need to accept that alcoholism is an illness and not a character defect. Most people believe that if the alcoholic practised self-restraint and controlled his drinking, then all would be well. They cannot understand why he cannot get a grip on his drinking. Although many of us number at least one heavy drinker among our friends, families, or colleagues, it is far more comfortable to think of the skid-row type of alcoholic and imagine him to be the typical alcoholic. The truth is that alcoholics come from all social classes, are usually in employment, and become parents. If you are not in too close a contact with them, they can appear to be otherwise normal; they just drink too much.

Most of the alcoholics I know, drinking or not, are very nice people – full of charm and good humour. The idea that their drinking pattern and the resultant behaviour form an identifiable illness which can be successfully treated may seem difficult to accept, but it is an important contention of this book. If we treat alcoholism as an illness and encourage alcoholics to find recovery, we can end the stigma and attend to the suffering of the whole family – suffering which you, the reader, may have experienced and, indeed, may still be blighted by.

Influence of advertising

Twenty-eight thousand people lost their lives in 1990 as a consequence of drinking – according to Alcohol Concern, the main national body concerned with drinking habits in the UK – yet advertisers continue to promote alcohol with minimal constraints. The images they project suggest that alcohol makes you cool, and fun to be with. Although such advertising is not supposedly aimed at young people, nor at promoting the idea that alcohol and sexual attractiveness are linked, or that excessive drinking is desirable, my work with young people aged 14 to 16 suggests that they *are* reached and excited by alcohol advertising. In my view, alcohol products need to carry health warnings and advertising should be severely restricted. We need to be informed about alcohol's effects on health and social behaviour and dispel forever the myth that 'the only person who is harmed by excessive drinking is the drinker'.

A typical example of how excessive alcohol consumption is promoted is the series of posters advertising a brand of rum. The scene is a beautiful Caribbean island, the caption reads: 'THIS IS WHAT PECKHAM LOOKS LIKE ON A SATURDAY AFTERNOON, IF YOU DRINK *******'. How much ********* must be consumed to achieve this effect? Surely not one or two glasses. What does Peckham look like on the Sunday morning after? Who was looking after the kids, and how were they affected?

More damaging, perhaps, is the message that if you are feeling down (the Peckham effect), then alcohol offers an acceptable escape to make you feel better. What does this message say to you about responsible, sensible drinking? And is it any surprise that having problems with drinking, or living with someone who is drinking, can be so difficult to articulate? It can be difficult to be alert to, or cognisant of, the suffering caused by excessive drinking in the context of such promotion. Today, young people are warned that 'heroin really screws you up'. Wouldn't it be helpful if they were told 'Alcohol really screws you up, too'? If you are the adult child of an alcoholic, wouldn't that kind of warning have encouraged you to confide in someone 'safe' and get help? – see Chapter 6.

The nature of alcoholism

In Chapter 1 I will give a more comprehensive definition of alcoholism but here it is sufficient to define an alcoholic as someone who will go to any lengths to obscure the connection between his drinking and the consequences. A simple example of this is the person who rings in to work on Monday morning (or gets a spouse to) with the excuse that he ate a 'dodgy curry' the previous evening and is now sick in bed. This is not to imply that everyone who uses this excuse after having drunk too much is an alcoholic, but rather that this behaviour is typical of the alcoholic. It is likely that the alcoholic believes that it was the curry and not the drinking which made him ill; the non-alcoholic knows that it was the drinking, even though he does not want to admit it.

Because the alcoholic systematically seeks to break the connection between his drinking and its effects, he needs those who are close to him to collude in his self-deception. His spouse and children are cajoled, frightened or terrorised into protecting him from the consequences of his drinking and, therefore, begin to deny that his behaviour has an impact on them.

As the illness progresses and it becomes more difficult to deny the connection between the drinking and its consequences, the alcoholic employs minimisation and delusion. If bad things happen – for instance, a job is lost because of absenteeism and poor work performance – he blames the boss, says he didn't want the job anyway and is better off away from it (delusion). Furthermore, he doesn't understand why his family is so upset about the loss of job and income (minimisation). Because he is angry and miserable about how tough life is on him, and how his family doesn't understand or love him, he turns to yet more drink for solace. His drinking appears to be in response to his job loss but the truth is that it was lost because of the drinking. Such is the nature of alcoholism. Not only are the effects of drinking hidden, denied, minimised, but the effects on the family, and particularly the children, remain obscured and unvoiced. Perhaps this is part of your experience.

The professional's response

If the alcoholic ever does become involved with a professional such as a doctor, psychiatrist or even a specialist alcohol agency (and this is unlikely because only about 5% of all problem drinkers are treated directly or openly for their problem), then *his* drinking becomes the focus of attention. It is highly unusual for the whole family to be assessed for the effects on them of his drinking behaviour. Thus, the problems of the spouse and children are not taken into account and remain hidden. That does not mean, however, that you must resign yourself to keeping your needs concealed, even in adulthood. But you have to go in search of help, as described later in this book.

The limited role that the professional plays, simply reflects the limitations forced upon him or her by slim resources. And so long as s/he is asked to refrain from intervention beyond that of trying to limit harm to the drinker's health and wellbeing, then s/he has little incentive – beyond a moral or ethical imperative – to extend his or her focus to the whole family. Children, of course, whether they are children of alcoholics (COAs) or not, have little choice but to endure what is meted out. They have limited legal standing or power to act as their own advocate. Their protection and nurture is dependent on the responsibility adults take for their welfare. Unfortunately, in alcoholic households the protection and nurture offered to children is variable, because such households revolve around the alcoholic and the vicissitudes of his drinking and related behaviour.

The typical adult child of an alcoholic would more likely see their parent's drinking as being the result of other problems: 'He drank to drown his sorrows', or 'she needed to drink because of all the pressures she was under'. Have you been given this kind of rationalisation in childhood? Perceiving drinking in this way not only supports the belief system operating within the alcoholic family but probably matches the belief systems of most people who come into ontact with them, including the family doctor, psychiatrist or scial worker who may be involved when the drinking problem gets out of hand.

The children's situation

The children of alcoholics prefer to remain unnoticed partly because of society's insensitivity towards alcoholism. The stigma involved means there is a far greater incentive to cover up and deny problems than to seek help. Where problems *are* noticed by outsiders, it is likely that, initially, they will not be thought to be connected to parental drinking. In Chapter 2, I will highlight the sort of problems that arise.

Mostly, children of alcoholics reject the idea that their father or mother could be an alcoholic – let alone that they themselves might be affected – because of how alcoholism affects family communication, which, as you'll learn in Chapter 3, becomes distorted and dysfunctional, and children consequently learn not to discuss or even to have feelings about the drinker's behaviour. Children of alcoholics, more than most, hold their family reputation in very high esteem and reject even the slightest imputation that all is, or was, not well. They feel a great need to protect the drinker, and to do so, will go to desperate lengths, often sacrificing their own interests and development.

As a society, we are very resistant to delving below the surface image of the drinker as a jolly, slightly mischievous character. How much more difficult it is for his children to claim that they have been damaged emotionally by such a nice person. Yet before the children can be fully helped, the destructive and disruptive nature of alcoholic behaviour must be acknowledged. Children need help and encouragement to speak out and reveal the true situation. Those of you who begin reading this book out of curiosity, rather than because you are an adult child of an alcoholic (ACA), may find yourself becoming more perceptive, and ready to help children that you might know who think they are 'wrong' to be distressed by the behaviour of the 'jolly' parent.

Even as adults, children of alcoholics feel as though they are a whining nuisance to everybody if they want to tell their story. Nobody has ever really convinced them that they are worthy people with a right to have and express their own feelings. They are used to 'shutting up and putting up'.

Facing up to the problem

This book is both for and about those who are facing up to the legacy of familial alcoholism. In Chapter 1, alcoholism is explained in relation to codependency, the general term used to describe the social and emotional context in which alcoholic families develop. Chapter 2 looks at the developmental consequences for children growing up in such families and the factors which seem to determine the severity of the effects of parental drinking. Chapter

3 describes how communication is distorted within the family system. Chapter 4 looks at children of alcoholics in adulthood and some of their common characteristics and dilemmas. Chapter 5 examines adult development and how it is affected by the family legacy of alcoholism. Chapter 6 is about stopping the rot and entering recovery. Chapter 7 describes the stages of recovery and includes advice on what to do if you feel that you've become stuck at any point. Chapter 8 evaluates the various aids to recovery, including self-help groups and professional services. It also introduces the idea of spiritual recovery and suggests some exercises. The final chapter suggests ways in which we can all help the adult children of alcoholics, if we have had the luck to escape such experiences ourselves.

I will present factual evidence, based on scientific research, and on people's stories told during therapeutic sessions and elsewhere, but always in a way that protects the identity of the individual concerned. Both sorts of evidence are important. Scientific facts about children of alcoholics are very few but have been gathered under strictly monitored conditions. As a consequence, they may seem narrowly focused, because so little of human experience is truly amenable to such methods. Anecdotal evidence is important because people are helped by telling their story and because we are concerned with human experience, but this type of evidence is, by its nature, selective, biased, and highly subjective. My hope is that, even so, the book will stimulate both sceptic and advocate alike.

Whether you have been affected by the drinking of another, or have come into contact with the problems associated with excessive drinking, or are simply curious, I ask you to consider your views on how alcohol use can and does affect families, and to revise your beliefs if this seems appropriate. I know that for many, the difficulty of reading this book and the resistance it may provoke will not be due to intellectual scepticism but, rather, due to the slow and painful realisation that it is about them and their own past and present. There is a resource section at the end giving telephone numbers and addresses of those who may be able to offer further advice, information and support.

Throughout, you will find that where there is reference to 'the alcoholic' I have used the masculine terms 'he' or 'his'. Of course, alcoholics can be male or female, but I have used the masculine form mainly because where the man is the alcoholic the family is more likely to stick together through thick and thin. The wife, partly for economic reasons is less likely to be able to leave. Where the wife is the alcoholic, she is more likely to be deserted. On the whole, children of alcoholics are addressed directly as 'you'. Professionals are referred to as 's/he'.

Finally, I hope to inform and enlighten you not from a spirit of knowing all about my subject but rather from the dictum that 'the teacher teaches mostly what he needs to learn himself'. My interest in children of alcoholics is not a purely professional one. It reflects a personal search to understand the impact of events in my own formative years. My father's drinking greatly affected me as a child, and the capacity of my family to function well. His premature death deprived him of the chance of recovery and the joy he could have known, and we could have shared together.

I would like you, the reader who is the child of an alcoholic, to know that beyond the sea of despair and the aching pain of loss and emptiness is a land of hope, joy and fulfilment, and ultimately peace of mind. The path is not an easy one, neither is it traversed speedily nor in a straight line. But you are not alone, and there is a great deal of help at hand. Robert Louis Stevenson once wrote that a successful life is not achieved by being dealt a good hand, but rather by playing a poor hand well. We cannot begin by asking for the deck to be reshuffled, nor will complaints about the dealer get us very far. Let us begin the book as we must begin recovery, by appreciating, in Chapter 1, the nature of alcoholism.

CHAPTER 1

Naming the Beast: Alcoholism

ONE of the major problems for children of alcoholics is coming to terms with the concept of alcoholism. It has such negative connotations that even many professionals, such as doctors and psychiatrists, opt for less controversial descriptions – problem drinker or alcohol dependence syndrome – because these are less value-laden. However, when the concept of alcoholism is thus dispensed with, vital aspects of the disease are minimised or denied. You may not be responsible for your parents' drinking, but you can be responsible for your own recovery. For this to succeed it is important to understand what alcoholism is, how it affects your parents, and how predisposed you may be. Intervention can then take place at any point.

When we talk about 'problem drinking' the implication is that we are talking about a purely behavioural disorder which could be remedied simply by altering drinking behaviour. This is patently not the case, as we shall see later in this chapter. 'Alcohol dependence syndrome' implies that we are dealing with a psychological or mental dysfunction, which could be remedied by an adjustment in beliefs, attitudes, or feelings. This, too, is an impoverished definition. Even if we use a narrow definition of disease, we imply that we are dealing with a purely physical, genetically based disorder which might be remedied by drugs or by genetic engineering. This view, too, would miss the point.

Furthermore, each of these terms fails to acknowledge the way alcoholism extends its destructive powers beyond the individual drinker into his family.

So what is alcoholism? What is it that so profoundly disturbs the functioning of whole families, having dramatic and detrimental effects on the development of children, and being passed down from generation to generation?

Every one of us is potentially an alcohol addict, because alcohol is an addictive substance quite unlike most others. It has particular characteristics which alter mood and experience, and induce us to continue consumption. Laboratory animals have become alcohol-dependent and can be bred to 'crave' alcohol. In humans, if taken in sufficient quantity and over periods of time, alcohol can alter brain chemistry and functioning in important ways. Ultimately, it can destroy the central nervous system and its vital organs, and lead to death. Critically, alcohol damages the precise centres of the brain that need to function well in order to recognise when alcohol consumption is a problem.

Scope of alcohol problem

According to the UK Standing Medical Advisory Committee, 1989, alcohol misuse is at least as common as diabetes, chronic bronchitis, or coronary heart disease. In Britain, 1.5 million people drink at levels which are definitely harmful (50 units a week for men, 36 units a week for women), while 7 million people drink more than is now regarded as sensible (21 units a week for men, 14 units a week for women). The Royal College of General Practitioners (1986), estimated that each GP has about 55 patients who drink at dangerous levels, 200 who drink at moderate levels and a further 1,150 who are vulnerable to drinking at risky levels.

The Medical Council on Alcoholism, 1987, reported that 62% of patients admitted to hospital with a serious head injury have raised blood alcohol levels. They also reported that drinking is implicated in 20% of deaths by drowning and 40% of deaths by fire. Millions of working days are lost each year because of alcohol induced sickness. A survey of admissions to York District Hospital found that 18 to

20% of men, and 2 to 4% of women had alcohol-related problems.

Of battered wives, 50% are victims of their husband's drunkenness, and alcohol is cited in over one-third of all divorces in the UK. There are also about 100,000 convictions for drunkenness offences each year, and a similar number of convictions for drink driving. Many crimes, particularly assaults and murder, are closely related to excessive drinking. According to Alcohol Concern, in the past year 28,000 people lost their lives as a consequence of alcohol misuse, and alcohol-related illness cost the nation over £2,000 million.

There is also evidence to suggest that alcohol-related problems are getting worse. According to the Medical Council on Alcoholism, 1987, deaths from liver disease almost doubled between 1970 and 1987, and cancer of the oesophagus and pancreatitis (inflammation of the pancreas) have increased markedly, both being indicators of alcohol-related illness and death.

However, it would be wrong to believe that all such problems result from alcoholism. Many who abuse alcohol are not alcoholic. They may, however, abuse alcohol 'by accident', not having information about alcohol as a dangerous drug and not understanding its powerful mood altering qualities. Such people usually end up in some sticky situation, either breaking the law or being involved in an accident. The shock of realising where their intoxication has led them can be sufficient to moderate or stop further episodes of intoxication.

A typical teenage or early adulthood example, is waking up in a strange bed, apparently having had sexual relations with the person lying next to them, and neither remembering the person's name nor how they arrived at their present location. Unfortunately, with the ever present spectre of AIDS/HIV hanging over them, learning about the effects of alcohol in this manner may be too late.

It is also true that some people drink to relieve depression or other anxiety states and, although some will develop alcoholism and require a dual diagnosis, most will drink steadily at moderate levels for long periods without their drinking progressing in the way that characterises alcoholism. Usually, an experienced clinician can quickly assess whether underlying mental problems are driving the alcohol consumption or whether, as is the case with alcoholism, the depression is a result of excessive drinking.

Also, many alcoholics successfully hide their addiction and receive treatment for physical and mental problems without having their drinking discovered. Research suggests that doctors do not regard it as a priority to question patients about their drinking habits.[1] Thus, the true figure for the number of alcoholics would include many covert alcoholics not identified in official statistics. My estimate of the number of people addicted to alcohol in the UK is between one to two million alcoholics, with a further five to eight million individuals 'at risk', who continue drinking in ignorance of the dangers if they persist in consuming alcohol at their present level.

So what is an alcoholic? Let us look at some of the characteristics that define an alcohol addict. (The vast majority of us are likely to have had experience of two characteristics which define addiction to alcohol or other mind altering drugs.)

Tolerance and withdrawal

Tolerance simply means that, over time, the brain needs more and more of an addictive drug such as alcohol to achieve the same mood altering effect. Most of us will have experimented with alcohol in our teens, when a glass or two of wine, or a pint or two of beer, sufficed to make us quite intoxicated and merry. As we use alcohol more, however, we require a greater quantity to achieve the same effect; by the time we are in our late teens we might need three or four pints of beer. This is what is meant by the development of tolerance.

Withdrawal effects, too, are within the range of common experience. Most of us are aware of the adage 'hair of the dog that bit you', frequently proferred to those who are hungover from a previous evening's excessive drinking. The body has been made ill because alcohol is toxic and depressing. But if another drink is consumed, then the depression can disappear as the level of alcohol in the bloodstream is raised – thus giving a lift to our mood and dispelling the withdrawal symptoms we were suffering.

Tolerance and withdrawal are of a different order in the later stages of alcoholism, but the same principles apply. An alcoholic is someone who progressively needs more and more alcohol to achieve a state of mood alteration, until he is drinking not to feel better but rather to avoid feeling so bad. At this stage, lack of alcohol creates nausea, an anxiety state, visual and/or audio hallucinations, severe shaking, and possibly lethal fits. It is not advisable, therefore, for an alcoholic to stop drinking by himself; he will need medical supervision if these withdrawal effects are to be managed adequately.

The disease entity and the disease concept

If alcohol is addictive, then why is it that everybody does not become chronically addicted and need more and more of the substance to diminish withdrawal effects and achieve mood alteration? The answer is that some people, by virtue of their biological makeup, react differently to alcohol than others. In the same way that some people have an allergy to penicillin – because there is something different in their biological makeup – so it is with alcohol. Some nervous systems treat alcohol in a quite different way from others. Quite simply, the majority – if not all – alcoholics are biologically different from the 'normal' population. This concept is vital to the argument that alcoholism is a disease.

We live in exciting times, as far as the study of the genetics of alcoholism is concerned. It would seem to be only a matter of time before we will know with greater certainty how alcoholism is transmitted genetically from one generation to the next. In 1990, Noble & Blum[2], analysing DNA from brain tissue (the building block of cells), found that the presence of a specific dopamine receptor (dopamine is a brain chemical critically affecting mood) correctly classified 77% of alcoholics, and its absence classified 72% of non-alcoholics.

Although such research needs to be pursued further, in order to confirm or refute this finding, it indicates how far research has progressed, identifying exactly what is different in the brain of an alcoholic and consequently explaining what alcoholics have been telling us for years: that something happens to them when they begin drinking which is different from the experience of non-alcoholics. 'I can't seem to get a grip. In fact, the more I try, the worse my drinking becomes.' Let us look at further evidence pointing to genetic and biological factors.

Inherited aspects

The incidence of alcoholism is not randomly distributed in the population. There is a high likelihood of inheritability, chiefly depending on two factors:

● The greater the number of alcoholics in the family history, the greater the chances of someone developing alcoholism in the present generation.

● The more closely you are related to an existing alcoholic, the more likely it is you will develop alcoholism.

Studies of fraternal and identical twins raised in their own homes are interesting in this respect, because identical twins have about twice as much genetic material in common as do fraternal twins. When one fraternal twin is an alcoholic, in 30% of cases his twin is also found to be an alcoholic, but with identical twins the co-occurrence figure is 60%[3] – which is highly suggestive of an inherited genetic factor.

More compelling evidence arises from adoption studies. Findings from studies conducted in Denmark and Sweden, in the early 1970s, showed that when sons of alcoholics are adopted by non-alcoholic families, they are just as likely to become alcoholic when they grow up as are those reared by their biological families. They are four times more likely to develop alcoholism than their peers in the general population, the same rate of risk as if they had been brought up in alcoholic households.

Children who are adopted run no greater risk of developing alcoholism by virtue of being adopted, so adoption *per se* does not account for these differences. In fact, whether adopted or not, 25% of the sons of alcoholic fathers develop alcoholism, according to American researchers. The greatest single predictor of alcoholism – in a son – is alcoholism in a father. Studies of daughters of alcoholic parents are less clear cut, but the indications are similar.

None of this research proves that alcoholism is genetically inherited. It could be that what is inherited is some more general character trait or temperament which leads to compulsive or anti-social behaviour, of which excessive drinking is but a part. The statistics are stark, but a knowledge and understanding of your vulnerability is the first step to take to ensure that you do not fit the pattern. Let us now look at some of the specific biological differences demonstrated in alcoholics, suggesting concrete, measurable ways in which they differ from others.

Biological differences

One of the difficulties in establishing biological differences between alcoholics and non-alcoholics was knowing whether differences discovered were, in fact, caused by the effects of alcohol. Children of alcoholics have become the focus of study because, in childhood, they have not yet begun to drink – yet they share common genetic material and are at high risk of developing alcoholism later. Therefore, looking at these children – who have not yet consumed alcohol – demonstrates differences that are not the effects of chronic alcohol use.

An instrument called an electroencephalogram (EEGs) measures total brain activity and, in 1984, a scientist named Henri Begleiter made an important discovery[4] when he identified a specific brain irregularity that is characteristic of alcoholics: the P3 brainwave relating to attention and learning was deficient in alcoholics. He decided to test the P3 brainwaves of a number of seven to 13-year-old sons of alcoholic fathers. These boys, with no previous alcohol use, were connected to electrodes and asked to make simple decisions about a picture of a head displayed at various angles. As they pushed buttons to indicate their choices, Begleiter measured the voltage of the P3 wave, and 35% of the boys showed a similar P3 deficiency – a deficiency that exists in very few children in general. These experiments provided the first neurological evidence that a specific, probably genetically determined, irregularity exists in both alcoholics and their non-drinking offspring.

Another scientist, Schukit[5], 1985, carried out a large number of tests across a wide range of variables, to test the reactions of sons of alcoholics, compared with sons of non-alcoholics, to the ingestion of various amounts of alcohol. His research shows that sons of alcoholics feel less intoxicated, experience less effect on their muscle control, and secrete less cortisol and prolactin (hormonal response chemicals), than the sons of non-alcoholics. Such research suggests differences in biological response to alcohol, and supports the theory that there *is* something different about alcoholics in their genetic and biological makeup.

I would suggest that this leaves us with a strong reason to believe that some, if not all alcoholics, for biological reasons, have difficulty in handling alcohol in a normal way. Before *any* alcohol is ingested they are at a disadvantage. Let us look at how these disadvantages are compounded by drinking alcohol, and some of the ways in which the disease of alcoholism progresses.

Physical effects

Excessive alcohol consumption effects important organs of the body: the liver, heart, kidney, and muscles, are all damaged or destroyed. The part of the body most crucially affected is the brain; excessive drinking causes peripheral nerve damage, memory loss – and dementia. It also affects the ability to feel emotion and even to think. And these aspects more than any others affect the capacity to develop and sustain intimate relationships, and to nurture children.

One of excessive drinking's more subtle and least understood effects on the brain is that of frontal lobe damage. These parts of the brain are thought to be the seat of high level mental functioning, including the ability to abstract, make judgements and abandon one perspective of a problem in order to adopt a different one from which new solutions are possible. In a variety of tests many alcoholics who are no longer drinking have been found to continue to suffer from damaged frontal lobes.

A probable consequence of impaired frontal lobes is that rigid thinking and denial are likely, thus impairing the capacity to make realistic judgements about one's own drinking or its consequences. Therefore, many alcoholics who appear to be excessively obstinate and obstructive to shifting views and facing the consequences of their drinking may be manifesting brain damage. Cermac,[6] 1990, describes the alcoholic with frontal lobe damage as being like a blind man who can't see how to get to the eye clinic, or a man with a broken ankle who can't walk to the emergency room. The very tool the alcoholic needs to use in order to get help is damaged.

Cermac writes: 'It can be useful for ACAs (adult children of alcoholics) to learn how cunning, baffling, and powerful the effects of alcohol on the brain really are. Then it no longer makes sense to say that their parents "should have been able to see" the damage they were doing with their drinking. Once ACAs accept that their parents may have been incapable of this, they can start drawing a more realistic picture of the past. That picture may contain a parent who was even more overtaken by alcohol than the ACA ever suspected.'

A further factor which most children of alcoholics find baffling while growing up, is the phenomenon of mood swings. Alcohol is mood altering. While intoxicated, parents are quite different from one moment to the next: jolly and loving at one minute, angry and maudlin at the next. When experiencing withdrawal symptoms they can be anxious, psychologically withdrawn, and very touchy. Such physiological effects are normal even with moderate drinking. In 1984, a researcher named Birnbaum[7] asked two groups of women not suffering from alcoholism to rate the intensity of their mood swings throughout the day, while one group totally abstained from alcohol, and the other group had up to two drinks a day, three days a week. When mood ratings were compared for those days upon which neither group drank, the drinkers had significantly higher highs and lower lows. If such relatively moderate amounts of alcohol can affect the brain and thus mood, then it takes only a small leap of imagination to see how the alcoholic who is drinking greater amounts is regarded as behaving in a sick or irrational way, and truly to be in the grip of a disease process.

A further way that alcohol effects the brain is in the occurrence of blackouts – not loss of consciousness but loss of memory. Many people have experienced waking up after drinking too much and finding that they cannot remember a part of the previous day. This is a blackout. One alcoholic I know, woke up one morning to discover he had got married in the course of a drinking binge which had lasted many days. He did not recognise his wife, nor did he have any memory of the wedding. This is a rather extreme example, but you can imagine the effect on children of a parent who has no memory of what has taken place the previous day – particularly as dramatic events frequently happen when the parent is intoxicated.

The argument that alcoholism is an hereditary based disease which predisposes the brain to react differently in the presence of alcohol, thus accounting for alcoholic behaviour, is persuasive. And it leads to hopes that through genetic screening or simple blood testing, alcoholics can be identified and cured by drug treatments, surgery, or some other mechanical means. But this view might be over optimistic. To understand why, let us achieve more perspective.

Genes and environmental factors

Research in the field of genetics, particularly in the field of intelligence and cognitive development, strongly suggests that there may be relatively few genetic 'givens', in the sense that environment has no effect upon them. Indeed a great deal of research is involved in understanding 'switching mechanisms' in our genes – what it is that causes some genes to be switched on and others not, and how the timing of this works. We may all carry genes responsible for a whole range of conditions, including alcoholism. But how, why, and when do these become activated in some individuals and not in others?

It is likely that there is a high degree of interaction between genetic and environmental factors. Even the brain grows and develops in our early years not purely on the basis of 'genetic programming', but is crucially affected by environmental feedback. For example, infants and children who are stimulated and intellectually challenged show more intelligence than those who are not. They also show a greater development of physical connections in the brain.

We also know that children with aggressive and anti-social temperaments, once thought to be genetically inherited, can be affected by change in diet and/or social conditions. This strengthens arguments for interactive effects between genes and environment. It appears that genes, in order to find expression, may need feedback from the environment, and the very structure of the brain is critically affected by the environment in which the child grows. Thus, in the case of alcoholism, the question is far more complex than whether one is born with a particular gene set or another.

Also, as you will discover later in this chapter, when I introduce you to some Scottish youngsters living with alcoholic parents, there are different types of alcoholic. And, although all alcoholics probably have more in common than they have differences, these latter are far from negligible, prompting some experts to argue that alcoholism, like cancer, is a family of diseases rather than a single one.

It is also true that the more alcohol is consumed by a society, the more alcoholics will be found there. This leads to the suggestion that some alcoholics are born alcoholics while others become or 'are made' alcoholics because of exposure to excessive drinking, or the social environment created where excessive drinking is common.

My view is that alcoholism is neither caused by a genetic predisposition nor by environmental factors. It is a highly complex condition which straddles our physical, mental and social being. To understand alcoholism requires far more than an appreciation of genetic factors; we need to place equal emphasis on our human strivings and our search for meaning and relationships. In this respect, poets, artists and philosophers have much more to teach us about the human condition and its relation to mind-altering substances than the rather mechanistic view of the biological scientist. There has always been, and there will probably always be, a creative tension between ideas of mechanism and ideas of meaning in understanding human lives in all their complexity.

Alcoholism – a disease of mind and emotion

Let us move on from the eternal organic factors in alcoholism to the idea of disease as a concept, and as a metaphor for the progressive nature of alcoholism. Psychology and psychoanalysis have offered important interpretations and explanation for alcoholism, and greatly help us to understand the disease.

One such expert, Levin[8], highlights characteristics which are common to active alcoholics: 'Impulsivity, inability to delay gratification, low affect tolerance [dislike of strong feelings], a propensity towards panic level anxiety and prolonged depression, and an unclear, confused sense of identity.'

In *Codependency*, 1991, Liz Hodgkinson and I proposed

that underlying alcoholism and other addictions was codependency, a condition characterised by low self-esteem, poor identity formation, and an excessive reliance on denial, and control of others to ensure psychic stability. Cermac puts it in a more sophisticated way for the professional reader. He formulates codependency as a specific character disorder closely related to what are called narcissistic character disorders. Indeed, he suggests that codependency and narcissism are mirror images. To those of you who are familiar with the Greek myth of Narcissus, psychoanalysts have emphasised the character of Narcissus, the one who fell in love with his own image; Cermac argues that the character of Echo, who fell in love with Narcissus, but could only respond to him in words that he gave her, is the archetypal codependent.

Vaillant,[9] 1977, describes alcoholics as people who have never really grown up. They are the 'adult children' described in so many recovery books. Attention has been drawn to the adolescent way in which alcoholics behave. Alcoholics have been consistently found to be field dependent. Field dependence means a particular way of organising one's experience of the outside world in which the environment assumes an inordinately important role. In other words, alcoholics are influenced more than most by peer pressure.

Jellinek's theory

E.H. Jellinek is perhaps the single most important theorist on alcoholism as a disease. In 1952 he described over 40 specific symptoms of alcoholism, and placed them along a continuum, from normal to alcoholic drinking. He has been particularly influential in plotting the development of alcoholism, which he believes has four distinct stages:

1: Pre-alcoholic phase

This is characterised by what we would call social drinking, that is, drinking to relax.

2: Early alcoholic phase

At this point, the drinker has his first blackouts, may become defensive about drinking and feel guilty about it. In this phase, the characteristic sneaking of drinks begins. The alcoholic makes sure that he orders the drinks so that extra ones can be consumed, 'just while I'm waiting'. He always has the first empty glass and becomes impatient with companions who are 'drinking too slowly'.

3: Addiction phase

The alcoholic is now physically dependent. He experiences loss of control over his drinking and his mounting financial and relationship problems become a rationale for further drinking.

4: Chronic alcoholism

In this final stage, the organs of the alcoholic's body are now being badly damaged, and he might die or become incapacitated by liver damage or heart disease. The brain is being steadily pickled and delirium tremens, alcoholic psychosis, or some other brain dysfunction may deprive the drinker of his sanity and, eventually, life itself.

The disease may progress slowly in some individuals. They may remain in the early alcoholic phase for 20 to 30 years, or it may be only two or three months before they progress to the addiction phase. What is clear, is that the disease progresses unless the drinker becomes aware of the problem and takes remedial action.

If the alcoholic is in the phase of addiction, then most experts agree that only complete abstinence will reverse the physical and mental decline. However, there is dispute as to whether abstinence is the only option for the alcoholic in the pre-alcoholic phase; some evidence suggests that controlled drinking is possible at this stage. But others argue that the control will ultimately break down in the face of a crisis, that the disease process is being stalled rather than arrested, and that abstinence is the only safe way of tackling the problem. Even if they are wrong and controlled drinking is possible, they argue, what harm has been done? The drinker will be fitter, healthier, and financially better off, for their 'mistake'.

Jellinek and later Max Glatt in the UK suggest that as the disease progresses, behaviour invariably spirals downward through the development of tolerance and physical dependence to the loss of control. At the same time the drinker's denial gradually deepens and becomes more rigid. However, there is hope and the disease idea charts not only the progression of the disease but also a mirror image progression of the process of recovery. It begins with the drinker breaking through denial and gradually repairing the damage to his/her life and eventually having full health restored. The only requirement is that the drinker refrains from taking any alcohol.

The family disease and codependency

Codependency is a general term used to describe certain types of family interaction which underlie various addictions, including addiction to alcohol. Let us look at Coates'[10] 1979 description of family interaction, which clearly illustrates how families progressively adapt to alcoholism and how the disease follows a parallel path in family members.

The alcoholic:

● Denies the alcohol problem, blames others, forgets and tells stories to defend and protest against humiliation, attack, and criticism from others in the family.

● Spends money on day-to-day needs for alcohol.

● Becomes unpredictable and impulsive in behaviour.

- Resorts to verbal and physical abuse in place of honest, open talk.

- Loses trust of family, relatives, and friends.

- Experiences diminishing sexual drive.

- Has feelings of despair and hopelessness.

- Thinks about suicide and possibly will make an attempt.

- Shows deterioration of physical health.

The spouse:

- Often tries to hide and deny the existing problem of the alcoholic.

- Takes on the responsibility of the other person, carrying the load of two and perpetuating the spouse's dependence.

- Takes a job to get away from the problem and/or maintain financial security.

- Finds it difficult to be open and honest because of resentment, anger, and hurt feelings.

- Avoids sexual contact.

- May over-protect the children, neglect them, and/or use them for emotional support.

- Shows gradual social withdrawal and isolation.

- May lose feelings of self-respect and self-worth.

- May use alcohol or prescription drugs in an effort to cope.

The children:

- May be victims of birth defects.

- May be torn between parents – in being loyal to one, they arouse and feel the anger of the other.

- May be deprived of emotional and physical support.

- Avoid peer activities, especially in the home, out of fear and shame.

- Learn destructive and negative ways of dealing with problems and getting attention.

- Lack trust in anyone.

- May lose sight of values, standards and goals because of the absence of consistent, strong parenting.

- Suffer a diminishing sense of self-worth as a significant member of the family.

This description of behaviour by family members living through active addiction can be shown to be progressive and to move through identifiable phases, defined by Ackerman.[11] See if they strike any chords for you.

1: *Reactive phase*

This phase is consistently dominated by the behaviour of non-alcoholic family members reacting to the alcoholic's behaviour. During this time, most family members are extremely cautious in their behaviour, in order to avoid further complicating the existing problems of alcoholism. They constantly adapt their behaviour in order to minimise or survive an unhealthy situation. Unfortunately, much of this 'adaptation' will not only have detrimental effects on them, but will also indirectly allow and support the continuing alcoholism. During the reactive phase, three typical family characteristics emerge. These are family denial, coping strategies, and social disengagement.

Family denial The entire family system denies the problem, possibly because family members do not want to admit that one of them is an alcoholic or because they perceive alcoholism as a reflection upon themselves. For example, they may fear that outsiders will say 'she drove him to drink', or 'is it any wonder she drinks the way those children behave'. Therefore, so long as the problem is hidden, family members can avoid being blamed.

Not talking about the problem is a means of sheltering oneself from the situation. For example, the non-alcoholic spouse might say, 'I have to cover up because I want to protect my children.' This tends to mean that the situation is never discussed. Of course, the children cannot be protected by such a cover-up. Paradoxically, they are protected from getting any help for themselves. Perhaps this was your situation?

Also, family members see the drinker as the primary patient and do not recognise their own need for help, whether or not the alcoholic gets treatment.

Coping strategies Coping strategies by non-alcoholic members include hiding or marking bottles, refusing to buy alcohol, and avoiding the alcoholic and other family members – thus isolating themselves from the problems. Verbal coping mechanisms include nagging, threatening, and theatrical behaviour by family members to get the alcoholic to change his behaviour. These strategies never work because alcoholics become adept at making others feel responsibility for their drinking behaviour and eventually settle on the idea that, 'If only they would stop going on at me I would be all right.'

In the withdrawing of family members from interaction with others, children no longer invite their friends home, and the non-drinking parent rarely goes out with her spouse, in order to avoid embarrassing scenes or confrontations. Of course, this pushes the family into closer intimacy – and isolation from the outside world – and all the negativity that this implies. Some family members attempt to become non-feeling, that is, deny and minimise negative feelings to prevent further pain.

The level of tension and anxiety increases, which leads to redoubling of efforts to be non-feeling and non-communicative and isolation becomes the most 'comfortable' state of being. This is how the 'don't feel' rule is instigated. If, as a child, you manage to establish primary relationships outside the home you can achieve some sort of nurturing while the family atrophies in on itself, but there is always home to come back to.

Many families do not go beyond the reactive phase. They deny the problem drinker is alcoholic, they helplessly hope for recovery, or they passively participate in the family malaise.

2: Active phase

This phase is marked by a 'de-centring' of the family away from the drinking member, that is, not by changes in the alcoholic's behaviour but in the behaviour of family members. It is not clear how families move into the active phase. It tends not to be a conscious decision or a shift that is made for positive reasons. It is more often triggered when, for some reason, it becomes so unbearable to continue in the reactive phase that the family begins to behave in ways that are 'out of character'.

The non-drinking family members may become aware of the alcoholism and gradually realise that they do not have to live like this. They seek help and discover that they are not alone, and do not have to be. If they are fortunate enough to find the self-help group, Al-Anon, they will learn that they are not responsible for causing the drinking person's problem and that the family can have recovery for itself, whatever the drinker decides to do, or not to do – see Chapter 8.

The family begins to behave more 'normally' again, deciding that despite the alcoholic's continued drinking they are going to 'get on with their own lives'. This phase is enormously important to the children, because far more attention is paid to them, their school work, and interests. They may discover Al-Ateen – see Chapter 8 – the self-help group for teenagers affected by a parent's drinking. They may learn to talk about themselves and the problems they face, and share their relief that they are not the only family to be afflicted by alcoholism. The family is now ready to move into the third phase.

3: Alternative phase

This is a natural progression from the active phase, although some families move into the alternative phase without going through the active phase. The alternative phase is truly decision time. The characteristics of this phase are polarisation, separation, change, and family reorganisation.

Polarisation   This is the process which precedes separation. It can be long and drawn out, and extremely painful and damaging to the children, because the family system is on the verge of collapse by virtue of the loss of denial by family members. The marital situation begins to deteriorate rapidly. The still drinking alcoholic is in a fury because his support system is being withdrawn. He may issue verbal threats or become violent as he redoubles efforts to protect his addiction from the loss of its enablers.

The children get caught in the middle and suffer the dilemma of whether to take sides. It is a time of impending change and they experience confusion, fear, resentment, anger; and increased isolation. Under this real threat of separation, some alcoholics seek treatment for their addiction, but it is far more common that empty promises of reform are made in an attempt to 'trick' the family into not deserting. You may have been subjected to such treatment.

Separation   Separation is the only viable alternative for some families. The separation may bring relief but sometimes it is exchanging one set of problems for another. Ackerman comments, 'For many children, separation will be life without daily contact with the alcoholic. Even within the same family, this change may be greeted with different feelings. For younger children, the loss of the parental role is of more concern than the loss of the alcoholic parent, but for older children it may be the opposite. They may perceive that although they may be losing the parental role, it was lost anyhow . . . and that they will no longer be affected by all of the family alcoholic problems. Much of their reaction will depend upon how the individual family members perceive this change in their lives.'[11]

Change The process of change in the family is rarely smooth and without some trauma for all concerned. If a great deal of time is spent in the polarisation and separation stages, children may be damaged by the long drawn out battling and agonising acrimony. If it all happens too fast, they may feel anxious and depressed because the speed of events has passed them by.

Family reorganisation Once separation has occurred, the family begins to reorganise itself. This may be a stage of further growth and development for some, as a new life is built in recovery. Other families may have under-estimated the parenting and practical input of the alcoholic, despite his alcoholism. The spouse may resent taking on new responsibilities, and the children dislike having to share the extra work. The family will face 'ordinary' stresses and strains and may be disappointed that their new life is not as they imagined it might be. The alcoholic can no longer be blamed for everything that goes wrong.

In bewilderment and fear, the family may revert to blaming him for creating the situation in which 'they had to leave him' and responsibility for taking positive action be disowned. The family may end up experiencing the worst of both worlds. Separated from the source of the problem yet living on past resentments and bitterness, they have failed to break free. You may well know how depressing such a situation can be.

A further complicating factor for the reorganisation of the family is the probable continued contact with the alcoholic parent. He may use such contact to get at the non-alcoholic parent, the children becoming pawns in the parental battle.

4: Family unity phase

This final phase is reached by relatively few families, because it relies crucially on the alcoholic stopping drinking. Some families may go straight from the reactive phase to the family unity phase and the stages are not always traversed in linear order.

There are at least three concerns to be negotiated in the family unity phase: sobriety, the dry drunk, and family growth.

Sobriety   In itself, this will not cause family growth – in the same way that the family did not cause the drinking. Sobriety will only make family growth possible. At the beginning, many families go through a honeymoon phase. The drinking has stopped and the family is still intact. However, without the alcoholic or the drinking to blame for all the family ills, new coping mechanisms have to be found as the family discovers that all families have their problems, and that blaming the bottle has become a way of avoiding taking responsibility for a whole host of difficulties faced by any ordinary family, for example, rebellious teenagers.

In other families, it takes time before the new found sobriety can be truly believed. Families may prefer to wait and see rather than risk disappointment, if it all turns out to be a charade.

The dry drunk   When the only change that has taken place is that the alcoholic has stopped drinking, all the old ways of relating are rigidly adhered to, the same old tensions, anxieties and conflict persist. The family fails to grasp the enormity of the damage that has been caused to the fabric of family relationships during the drinking years.

The children find the sober alcoholic's attempts to parent strange and alien, because it is a new experience. In their fear, they may reject the parenting and display a preference to be left alone. Families who are on a 'dry drunk' may eventually need professional help to explore their new found freedom in a constructive way.

The alcoholic in recovery may be tempted either to return to drinking to relieve the family of the burden of its new potential, or seek to fulfil intimacy and sexual needs outside of the marital context – perhaps you recognise this in your family?

Family growth Family growth occurs for those families where the sober alcoholic is integrated into the fullness of family life. The family does not dwell on the past in a negative way. The past is a source of learning, neither to be avoided nor over-emphasised. Life becomes a journey and then an adventure together. There is a realisation that 'happy families' are built not upon the avoidance of conflict and pain, but rather on how conflict and pain is handled. If there is respect and love, then life with all its ups and downs can be faced together, with confidence. Many families who develop thus begin, in a spiritual way, to see the traumatic drinking times as an unfortunate and expensive way to have been brought to a realisation of their own emotional and spiritual impoverishment, and to understand themselves and become philosophical in a way that would not have been possible in the ordinary course of events.

Spiritual disease

Alcoholism has also been described as a spiritual disease, not merely because moral and ethical standards gradually decline as the drinking takes a grip, but also because the recovery of many alcoholics and their families does not take off until they have had what Alcoholics Anonymous calls a spiritual awakening. This is not to be confused with a religious experience, although for some the two are equivalent. The spiritual aspect will be discussed in Chapter 7.

Alcoholism, then, can be defined as a disease of the body, mind, and spirit, in which a person loses the capacity to consume alcohol in a controlled way. Its tentacles reach beyond the boundaries of the person into his social world and affect all who come into close contact – especially family members, to the extent that they suffer serious physical, mental, and spiritual problems. Once engaged, family members become part of the disease and are greatly harmed, despite the fact that no alcohol may pass their lips. The disease is multi-generational, has a genetic basis and real physical underpinnings for the majority, if not all sufferers. It cannot, however, be understood independently of the social context in which it manifests itself. There is no cure, only recovery.

Scottish teenagers speak out

Having defined alcoholism, let us now look at the disease in action – as described by some Scottish teenage children of alcoholics, who made a tape of their experiences for the Scottish Council on Alcohol, in 1990.

1. Binge drinking

John is the first to speak: 'You know, I do as much as I can around the house, but it's never enough. I make the tea for my mum, I wash my wee brother and put him to bed. I get him up in the morning and give him breakfast. But nothing seems to help. Everything I do is wrong. Sometimes my mum is brilliant, everything is good then, but then she goes on a binge and that's that. My dad just clears out. I saw him crying once; he didn't know I saw him, it scared me. Sometimes I get scared he will go for good. I don't know what we would do then.

'But you do feel it's your fault, I keep thinking, maybe if I did more in the house, my mum wouldn't get so mad at me. Maybe if I was better at school she wouldn't get mad at me. I try hard at school, but it's difficult to concentrate. Sometimes I even fall asleep. The teacher bawls me out or she sends a letter home and then I get it again. I used to like school, too. When I was wee my teacher thought I was good at some things, but it's got harder and I get really tired, and end up losing the place. Sometimes I "dog it" (play truant). At least, then, I can stay at home on my own and get some peace.'

John's mother is a 'binge drinker'. Binge drinking, that is periodic bouts of heavy drinking, is very much part of the pattern with some alcoholics. As the disease progresses the periods of bingeing come closer and closer together so that it becomes one continuous binge. However, the disease may remain in the bingeing phase for many years before a more continuous pattern emerges.

Let us listen now to Fred, whose father many of us might have difficulty identifying as an alcoholic. We might prefer to call him just a 'heavy drinker'.

2. *The 'ghost in the house' drinker*

Fred: 'My dad's not that bad, he just comes home dead drunk every night, sits in front of the telly and falls asleep. It drives my mum mad. She gets mad at him, and when he goes on snoring she gets mad at us. Some nights she gets so fed up she just goes to bed and leaves him. It's funny sometimes, it's as if he is not there. He hardly ever talks to us, he's like a ghost. My mum cries a lot and is always moaning at us ...

'Because I thought everyone knew my dad got drunk, I thought people pushed me aside. "His dad's a drunk, we don't want to have anything to do with him." I don't know if people really think that, but that's how you feel ... If I could tell someone I would. I'd like us to be like other people. I think my friend's mum knows about my dad. She is always nice to me when I'm at their house. The thing is I don't want people to feel sorry for me. I want someone to make it different, so we can be like other people.'

Fred's dad drinks to oblivion every night. He is physically addicted to alcohol and is likely to be causing great damage to all the organs of his body. In time, he is likely to develop an alcohol-related illness, and this may be the crisis which provokes him to stop drinking, or to escalate his drinking as he tries to comfort himself, because he has alienated his family and is a stranger to them.

Unlike Fred's dad, who we might think if we knew him socially 'wouldn't hurt a fly, a really nice, quiet chap', Morag's father is more like the wild drunk man we might be more used to thinking of as alcoholic.

3. The wild drunk

Morag: 'I don't know what else to do, I've tried things, but nothing seems to work. My dad's OK, but when he comes back from the pub it's unreal. I try to keep out of his way, but I always end up getting it. The thing is, I never know when it's going to happen. You just have to watch out all the time and wait for it coming ... So last week we had a parents' night at school, and my dad promised he'd come with me. My art teacher put some of my pictures on the wall. She said they were quite good.

'I wanted mum and dad to see them, but my dad got drunk again and just walked out in a bad mood. So I didn't bother going to school, there wasn't much point, was there? I didn't tell the teacher why they didn't come. Well, I couldn't could I? I just said they had something else to do. She wasn't very pleased. I think she thinks I didn't ask them. Sometimes, my dad can be great fun. He was like that when I was younger. It was great then, but it's not like that now.'

Morag illustrates the way in which children of alcoholics cover up for their parents. The truth is that her father is an alcoholic. His drinking is the most precious thing to him and he cannot see the consequences of his actions while he continues to drink.

Michael, below, describes a pattern that can occur when the non-alcoholic spouse decides, 'If you can't beat them – join them.'

4. The raving drunk

Michael: ' . . . there's other things that make you feel hopeless, too. You know, sometimes I think it would be great to bring my pals home. I've been to their houses and they can play records, watch the telly, and muck about, and nobody bothers too much. I can't bring anybody to our house, you never know what's going to happen with my mum. Sometimes my dad goes out drinking with her, too, and it's even worse then. They come home and fall about, and he gets mad at everybody. He starts shouting and things get thrown around. I usually end up getting a "doin" . . .

'Sometimes I think it would be great if somebody knew what it was like, that maybe things would change. But you can't tell anyone about it, can you? I think some of my pals know something is up with my family. But you don't want to talk about it. They are your mum and dad and you don't want to cause any hassle. There is enough hassle already. Sometimes I feel really lonely, you know, because I can't tell anyone what it's really like. I wish there was somebody and they really knew what it was like.'

Michael, too, is keeping the family safe from discovery so that no further hassle is caused. Children of alcoholics typically sacrifice their own safety and wellbeing in this way. Mary, below, describes another feature of alcoholism. As the drinking takes off, life can become chaotic and unmanageable.

5. The mercurial drunk

Mary: 'Sometimes I just give up. It's not knowing from one day to the next what's going to happen. She seems to change so fast. She gets her drink and starts off happy, and then she changes. She goes mental. The thing is that even is she weren't like that, I wouldn't want to bring pals home. Our house is a dump. I try as much as I can to clean things up but it's pretty hopeless. You see, she doesn't care anyway. Some days she keeps me off school to look after my wee brother, so she can go out drinking.'

The disease of shame

All these youngsters illustrate the shame and embarrassment felt because of having alcoholics as parents. It is as though they had given birth to their parents and caused them to drink in a shameful way, rather than being victims of the disease we know as alcoholism.

These small vignettes give some idea of the great variety of alcoholic types. Although they have many features in common, other features are quite distinct. Michael's father is physically abusive, whereas Fred's dad is like a ghost, neglectful and absent. If these youngsters have caused you to think of your family and how you might have been affected by another's drinking, then the following questionnaires could help you to assess how you might have been affected.

The first questionnaire was designed for use at an alcoholism treatment centre in the USA.[12] The questionnaire should be answered by any family member, spouse or child. If you are assessing how you might have been affected some years ago, when you grew up in a home where drinking was a problem, then just change the tense of the questions. Bear in mind that they are only useful if they are answered as honestly as possible, so make sure you answer them somewhere that is quiet and free from intrusions.

The Reddy questionnaire

- Do you lose sleep because of a problem drinker?

- Do most of your thoughts revolve around the problem drinker or problems that arise because of him?

- Do you exact promises about the drinking which are not kept?

- Do you make threats or decisions and not follow through on them?

- Has your attitude changed towards this problem drinker (alternating between love and hate)?

- Do you mark, hide, dilute and/or empty bottles of liquor or medication?

- Do you think that everything would be OK, if only the problem drinker would stop or control the drinking?

- Do you feel alone, fearful, anxious, angry and frustrated most of the time? Are you beginning to feel dislike for yourself and to wonder about your sanity?

- Do you find your moods fluctuating wildly as a direct result of the problem drinker's moods and actions?

- Do you feel responsible and guilty about the drinking problem?

- Do you try to conceal, deny, or protect the problem drinker?

- Have you withdrawn from outside activities and friends because of embarrassment and shame over the drinking problem?

- Have you taken over many chores and duties that you would normally expect the problem drinker to assume – or that were formerly his?

- Do you feel forced to try to exert tight control over the family expenditures with less and less success – and are financial problems increasing?

- Do you feel the need to justify your actions and attitudes and, at the same time, feel somewhat smug and self-righteous compared to the drinker?

- If there are children in the house, do they often take sides with either the problem drinker or the spouse?

- Are the children showing signs of emotional stress, such

as withdrawing, having trouble with authority figures, rebelling, acting-out sexually?

● Have you noticed physical symptoms in yourself, such as migraines, nausea, a 'knot' in the stomach, ulcers, shakiness, sweating palms, bitten fingernails?

● Do you feel utterly defeated – that nothing you say or do will move the problem drinker? Do you believe that he can't get better?

● Where this applies, is your sexual relationship with a problem drinker affected by feelings of revulsion; do you 'use' sex to manipulate – or refuse sex to punish him?

The Brooks questionnaire

Here is a further questionnaire[13] specifically for children of alcoholics to help assess their feelings about parental alcoholism. If you are an adult, then simply change the tense to the past:

● Do you worry about your mom's or dad's drinking?

● Do you sometimes feel that you are the reason your parent drinks so much?

● Are you ashamed to have your friends come to your house, and are you finding more and more excuses to stay away from home?

● Do you sometimes feel that you hate your parent when he is drinking, and then feel guilty for hating him?

● Have you been watching how much your parent drinks?

● Do you try to make your parent feel happy so he won't get upset and drink more?

● Do you feel you can't talk about the drinking in your home – or even how you feel inside?

● Do you sometimes drink or take drugs to forget about things at home?

- Do you feel if your parent really loved you he wouldn't drink so much?

- Do you sometimes wish you had never been born?

- Do you want to start feeling better?

By the end of this chapter, no doubt you understand some of the complexity of alcoholism and how devastating it can be to the whole family. If you are the child of an alcoholic, then I hope you have gained some helpful insights into the disease which has affected your life. It is time now to turn our attention to the children as they grow and develop in the alcoholic home, perhaps with further moments of self-recognition for you or better understanding of the past life of an acquaintance or close friend. Recovery is our aim.

CHAPTER 2

Growing Up in the Shadow of the Bottle

IN THE previous chapter several Scottish teenagers described how their lives are affected by their parents' drinking. Now we will look at the physical, mental and emotional development of children and how these aspects are affected by alcoholic parents.

Physical development

Children of alcoholic parents (and perhaps you were such a child) are prone to a number of physical problems stemming from parental alcohol abuse and its consequences. Even before you were born to an alcoholic mother you will have suffered a greater chance than most of your peers of developing a birth defect.

Before birth Excessive drinking during pregnancy can produce what is called Foetal Alcohol Syndrome (FAS). This results in the birth of children with irreversible physical under-development – lower than normal intelligence, retarded motor development, and a characteristic facial and bodily appearance of mild retardation. Yet, not only is FAS avoidable but children do not recover from it.

Even moderate amounts of alcohol affect the foetus and good medical advice counsels all mothers to abstain from alcohol use during pregnancy, or at least that its use is kept to a minimum. Many alcoholics use other drugs in addition to alcohol, including minor tranquillisers and tobacco, which also increase the risks to the foetus. Premature babies of lower than expected birth weight are often the consequence. Alcoholics can also manifest food disorders, which affect the balance of diet so important in childbearing. In particular, vitamin deficiencies can affect the mother's health and lead to illness which, in turn, affects the developing foetus. Even when there is no food disorder, most alcoholics neglect a proper diet.

Even where the alcoholic is the father of the child, the stresses often generated in an alcoholic household may affect the health of the foetus – if the mother is anxious, depressed, and emotionally abandoned, she is more likely to become ill and the foetus may be affected. If the family also suffers financial insecurity or housing problems then these compound the effects of alcohol drinking.

Childhood physical effects   Think back to your early childhood and the illnesses you or your brothers and sisters may have suffered. Children of alcoholics have been found to be more prone to migraine and asthma and to have sensory problems with noise, bright lights, heat and cold.[1] They are more inclined to allergies, anaemia, frequent colds or coughs, and to be overweight or underweight.[2] Of course, other factors are involved in each of these conditions but research studies suggest that they are associated with alcoholic parenting.

You may also have been inclined to feeding problems as an infant and you will have been more likely than most to cry incessantly and to vomit.[3] Later on in childhood you may have experienced abdominal pain, headaches, tiredness, sleep problems, tics, enuresis, and nausea, and no physical cause of these complaints will have been found.[3] Perhaps you have sometimes wondered about these childhood illnesses but never before associated them with alcoholic parenting. Or you may have been among the fortunate ones who suffered none of these complaints – alcoholic parenting is not the single cause of any of these problems but it is strongly associated with them.

There are important sex differences. Sons of alcoholics in one controlled study were found to have suffered 60% more injuries, were five times more likely to report emotional problems, and were two and a half times more likely to be classified as severely ill or disabled.[4] Daughters of alcoholics were hospitalised three and a half times more often than their peers and had three times more counselling sessions than other girls.[4]

Pre-school children of alcoholics (of either sex) are 65% more likely to be ill than other children.[4] If you are the child of an alcoholic you are five times more likely to have had a psychiatric examination than other children.[5]

Growing up in an alcoholic family is clearly hazardous to health and it would seem that children from such families place larger burdens than most on medical services.

Mental development

Children of alcoholics suffer from a range of psychological problems which affect their capacity to learn. For many people their school years are full of happy memories, but if you are the child of an alcoholic then this is less likely. In one study, children of alcoholic mothers at primary school did significantly less well at reading and maths than other children.[6] Another study showed children of alcoholic parents displaying all sorts of learning difficulties, changing school more frequently, more often repeating exams, and more likely to be referred to the school psychological service.[7]

In addition to these learning difficulties, children of alcoholics can display difficult and disruptive behaviour.

Troubled – and troublesome   It may not surprise you to learn that children of alcoholics are more likely than most to display behavioural problems at school. But it might surprise you to know that they have more problems even than children whose parents suffer from psychiatric illness. In one study, children of alcoholics were found to be more isolated, less able to maintain attention, more fearful, liable to emotional upset, and more preoccupied with inner thoughts than with the world around them.[8]

How was it for you at school? Were you a bit of a dreamer, cut off emotionally and isolating yourself, or were you more like those people described in the study which looked at the children of alcoholic fathers?[3]

Their teachers assessed that almost half (48%) were problem youngsters. Among boys aged seven to nine, 74% of the sons of alcoholics showed emotional instability and anxiety. They were also likely to be hyperactive and to have trouble concentrating.

However, as we shall see in the following chapter many children of alcoholics are neither disruptive nor troublesome. Indeed, they are the opposite – accommodating and sensible well beyond the norm. Their path of survival is through compliance and achieving to please.

In adolescence, the obviously troubled and troublesome ones continue to catch the eye. In one study[9] teenagers from alcoholic family environments were found to be twice as likely to receive psychiatric treatment for behaviour disorders and anxiety-depressive symptoms. A 20-year investigation of 259 problem children, of whom 144 were children of alcoholics, showed that 59% of those from alcoholic families did not finish school and dropped out due to early marriage, pregnancy, to join the army, or were expelled or institutionalised.[10]

So what might be done to offset these problems or to arrest the slow drift through one school problem to another? Ellen Moorehouse, on behalf of the National Association for Children of Alcoholics in the USA, 1989, compiled a list of behaviours a teacher might see in class that indicate the possibility that they are dealing with the child of an alcoholic. The list is included in Appendix 3, at the end of this book, as it might be useful to any adult who has temporary charge of children, whether as a youth leader, residential social worker or scout master.

Erikson's stages of development

Erik Erikson,[11] 1963, proposed a series of eight stages to characterise development from the cradle to the grave, the capacity to negotiate each stage being crucially affected by the successful completion, or otherwise, of the previous one. Erikson believes that emotional development is dependent upon the relationships established at various points in our life cycle, and that at each stage there are special problems or 'crises' to be negotiated and overcome. Here I will look at, and comment upon, the first five of these stages – relating to childhood and adolescence. The final three stages, negotiated in adulthood, are examined in Chapter 5.

See how they fit in with your own experiences, if you are the adult child of an alcoholic – or perhaps have a close relationship with one. The more you *understand* about your past, the easier it will be for you to take responsibility for your present and future recovery.

1: Trust versus mistrust

This stage is negotiated in the first year of life – and is perhaps the most important. A faulty negotiation will affect your capacity to negotiate all further stages. The key crisis to be negotiated is that of trust vs mistrust and your significant social relations are with mother or mother substitute. A favourable outcome to this stage is that you move into your second year with a basic sense that the world is a safe place which can be trusted and approached with optimism.

Family reorganisation   At the best of times the entry of a new baby into the family can be difficult. There is a loss of sleep, household routines are disrupted, and siblings may be reacting to the presence of the new baby. There may be many visitors to see the new arrival. There may be other less common problems, such as post-natal depression. It is a time of both elation, if the baby is wanted, and stress as the family is reorganised to accommodate the new member.

No parent ever manages this perfectly; the best that can be hoped for is that parents can become 'good enough'.

Providing continuity As the infant develops, the role of the parent is to provide continuity to the child's rather diffuse inner life, and his/her attempts to make sense of a mass of novel sensations and experiences. We are born with a capacity to gain attention for ourselves by crying and the capacity to suck in order to sustain ourselves, given a reasonably available caregiver. But it will be about six weeks before our eyesight can even focus properly upon our parents, and about 18 months before we will fully recognise that we are separate entities from them. Parents and other caregivers must be relatively consistent and present in order for us to have a sense of safety, otherwise we may be overwhelmed by anxieties about survival in a chaotic and threatening world.

Fear of abandonment It is argued that a child's crying is a vital evolutionary tool, without it we might be forgotten, abandoned, and die through lack of nourishment. The fear of abandonment and its consequence – death – is thought by many psychologists to be our most primitive fear. As we shall see, it is a fear which overwhelms many children of alcoholics and becomes 'the basic fault' in their adult relationships.

Narcissistic needs and codependency The first year is also crucially connected to healthy 'narcissism' or our love of ourselves. For if we come to believe that we might be abandoned because we do not receive consistent and adequate care – then we will later on doubt our worth as human beings. The need for constant reassurance and boosting will emerge, and thus we determine to 'make' others love us in the way we 'failed' to make our parents love us. This 'codependent' behaviour – attempting to control others in order to feel good about ourselves – is triggered by a wish to put right whatever went wrong in our infancy.

The alcoholic mother in the first year In the alcoholic household, many stresses impinge on a parent's capacity to meet the emotional needs of her infant. The alcoholic mother may have abstained from alcohol for a part or even the whole of her pregnancy. Now she perceives that it is 'safe' to resume drinking, and because her own anxieties are overwhelming, she does so with a vengence. Consequently, her capacity to respond sensitively to the cries of her baby are impaired. The child may be fed when it is in need of a nappy change or have a nappy change when it is in need of a feed. The mother may be intoxicated, hung over, suffering withdrawal, preoccupied with drinking, or sleeping it off, all of which take away from the considerable energy and commitment required of a 'good' mother.

The alcoholic father in the first year If you have an alcoholic father he may well have missed the birth itself because he was in the pub or otherwise unavailable. This will not have deterred him from 'celebrating' the birth with more drinks. Mother, meanwhile, is unsupported and faces the difficult task of caring for her new baby – you – alone. Without the support of a partner she is less able to be sensitive to you. She may also have to protect you from the excesses of her husband, whose natural jealousy may be magnified by the effects of intoxication.

Your father may insist on resuming sexual relations before she is physically or emotionally ready. He may become verbally or physically abusive to you for 'crying too much'. On other occasions he may wake you up to 'admire' you or be lavishly affectionate or 'teasing'. Your mother, if she protests at this behaviour is called silly or a spoilsport. She becomes distressed and fearful and this may be communicated directly to you in how you are handled or indirectly in the anxious atmosphere in which you are being nurtured. Your mother's stress is likely to affect her production of breast milk and may cut short the time you are breast-fed.

It may be that either parent hits on the idea that you should be given a little drop of brandy to get you to sleep or to stop crying. 'My mother gave it to me and it didn't do me any harm,' is the likely rationalisation. However, a baby's developing organs will not be helped by the introduction of a toxic substance such as alcohol. It might even exacerbate 'colic' and other digestive problems, or indeed cause you to be distressed, in which case your parent may respond with greater doses of alcohol, making things worse.

If this was your experience in the first year you are likely to have left this stage with an impaired sense of trust and an anxious or fearful attitude to yourself and others. Let us illustrate this with a case example.

Michael – who could not play with his children

Michael was 28 years old when he first consulted me about his depression. He was the second of five children from a working-class area in the North of England. His father was an alcoholic of the quiet 'ghost-like' variety, described in the previous chapter. He was a foreman at a local industrial plant, but he could have made a lot more of himself, according to Michael. He was bright and able enough but he just seemed content to do his job and to drink in the pub every evening, and most of the weekend. 'We saw him a bit on Sunday afternoon because the pub was closed 'til seven. Even then he watched telly and got annoyed if we played too loud.

'Once there was a strike at the factory, and he couldn't go to work for six weeks. There was very little money, so he couldn't go to the pub so often. He was like a bear with a sore head. I remember I brushed past him in his chair while he was sleeping once, he leaped up, shouted at me and lifted his hand to hit me. I was completely shocked and frozen to the spot. I remember the anger in his eye, then shock as he, too, realised that he was behaving out of character. I burst into tears, and he said he was sorry and tried to comfort me. I remember feeling delighted that he was giving me attention, but I could not show my happiness, in case he thought I had faked my upset. My mother arrived on the scene, and she, too, was crying. She gave him two one pound notes from her purse. He was gone two minutes later, and the incident was never discussed again, until just now when I told you.'

Michael seemed surprised that he had opened up to me. 'I didn't really want to see a psychotherapist, I feel a bit silly. You see my wife heard a talk you gave to some health visitors $his wife is a health visitor£, about alcoholism and the family. She thought that what you were saying was relevant to my problem, although I'm sure my father was not an alcoholic. He never touched spirits, and he never drank alone. He was just a hard drinking man. I came really because my wife thinks it can do no harm.'

I asked what he thought his problem was. 'It's hard to describe really – I've got two children who I really love but every time I play with them they end up crying and running to my wife, saying that I've upset them. Then *I* get upset and think I am useless as a father. So I don't play with the kids to avoid trouble, but that just makes me feel worse because I want to play with them. I wouldn't do anything to harm them. I see other children play with their fathers but I can't even read to my lot without the whole thing ending in tears.' His own eyes filled with tears. 'It's getting me down, I feel I'm being punished for a crime I haven't committed. I don't even know what the crime is. Does this make any sense to you?'

I told him that I thought there were important connections between how his father had been with him and how he was feeling about his own children. I said that I was moved by his plight and the way he had talked suggested that he might need to talk some more.

He looked quite surprised, but nodded agreement. 'Do you think my father was an alcoholic?' he asked (his father died, aged 47, of a heart attack). I said that I didn't know, but things he had told me were similar to what I had heard before from children of alcoholics. I asked if it mattered to him if his father *was* an alcoholic. He replied, 'No, I suppose it doesn't, but I need to know what's wrong with me, I need someone to make me right, and I don't give my trust easily.'

I said that I thought he was right not to give his trust easily to anyone, but that I was interested that he should make the statement about trust in such a general way. He added, 'Look, this really is not easy for me. I don't know how to answer your question.' I asked how that felt. He looked at me in anger. 'I don't know if I can continue.' He averted his eyes for the rest of the consultation.

Michael did not start therapy for a further seven months, though he came for three more consultations in the intervening period. On each occasion he said that he wished to start therapy, but by the end of the consultation felt that starting would be too difficult because he couldn't be sure he could trust me. On each occasion I told him that I did not expect him to trust me straight away and that if he decided to start therapy it would have to be on the basis that trusting me was so laden with difficult feelings that we would have to understand these feelings before trust could enter our relationship.

Michael, like many who have difficulty with basic trust, also had problems initially with therapy. (Sometimes, such patients engage in a superficial way for a while, and get better very quickly from their presenting symptoms, so as to avoid deeper contact.) However, in this case, he went on to complete his work with me, and we shall return to his story later.

Those who do face their fears about trusting others find that greater intimacy in relationships becomes possible and the quality of life improves immeasurably. They may still get frightened or anxious in the face of difficulties but they are no longer controlled by such fears. So if you find yourself struggling with developing trust, do persevere – it can take a little time before you get it right.

Not all children are affected in this very fundamental way. In many alcoholic families the drinking takes off when children are older and the early stages of development have been completed satisfactorily. Such children are more able to handle the onset of alcoholism in a parent. Their pain is still considerable but they have greater resources to bring to their recovery.

2: *Autonomy vs doubt*

In the second year of life you begin to move about on your own. You want to explore, investigate, and do things for yourself. To the extent that your parents encourage such activities, you begin to develop a sense of independence or autonomy, learn to control some of your impulses and to feel pride in accomplishments. Over-protection or over-controlling behaviour in parents or others that restricts what you are permitted to do, or ridicules unsuccessful attempts, may cause you to doubt your abilities. A good outcome of this stage leaves you with a sense of self-control and adequacy; a bad outcome leaves you anxious and impulsive, with an abundance of shame. Shame is a sense of your own 'badness'.

In my clinical experience, children of alcoholics have more problems with this stage than any other. In particular, it is because the child develops its sense of separateness that this stage becomes so problematic. As we have seen, both alcoholics and their spouses – in the grip of the family disease of alcoholism – have tremendous difficulty in seeing children as separate beings, with needs of their own. Alcoholic parents, inextricably imersed in their own narcissism (self love) and codependency (self-sacrificing other love) have often never really achieved true separateness themselves. Their marriage may have been a merger of sick roles, two people who cling together, simultaneously loving and hating each other.

Perhaps in your alcoholic family, you felt that there was no place for you. Your healthy development threatened the continuance of the family sickness, causing them to close ranks against you. This is devastating, for in our second year comes the realisation that we are separate beings from our parents and the world, that food, attention, and survival do not arrive by magic or as a 'right'. Rather, we become aware that they are provided by real people upon whom we are entirely dependent.

Healthy families In healthy families, our parents make adaptations so that we feel that they value and respect our individual demands and needs. Parents take pleasure in us and act as a sort of mirror to our joy and interest. Language is developing and our parents are interested in our utterances. Simultaneously, we begin to explore the world with our new found mobility. Our parents are able to exert control and restrictions in a consistent way to ensure our safety from potentially dangerous situations, such as falls and accidents.

By the end of the second year we feel valued and loved, for our sake, and able to exert some self-control in place of parental control. It must be stressed that in any family there are no perfect outcomes. All children have to adapt to their parents' or siblings' needs to some extent, but in healthy families the adaptations are made by all and, as far as possible, in the child's best interests.

Alcoholic families   In alcoholic families the situation is very different. The parents are unable to show flexibility in adapting to the needs of the child, and because of the nature of alcoholism and codependency, are likely not to have successfully negotiated this stage themselves, in childhood. Thus the quality of parenting reflects not the needs of the present child, but rather is a repetition of their own development in their own families, or a reaction against it.

If your family was like this, you were perhaps over-indulged or over-controlled. Your parents could be lavish in their attention or withhold it, or more commonly, they alternated between the two extremes. You may have been allowed to explore very dangerously, or not allowed to explore at all.

One single mother I interviewed, proudly told me that she always put her son in the play pen when she was drinking so that no harm could come to him if she passed out. A drinking bout usually lasted for three or four days, during which time her son was confined, without adequate stimulation or contact. I learned that she, too, was the child of an alcoholic – her father. Her mother used to confine the children to their bedroom when their father was at home to protect them from his drunken violence.

Defective mirroring The emotional impact of parents who repeat or react against their own childhoods in their behaviour towards their children, is severe in this second stage of development. In order to feel valued and loved, as children we must feel recognised as unique and worthy of attention in our own right; otherwise we are faced with a reversal of roles in which we act as a mirror to our parents' own childhood experiences. Alcoholic and codependent parents have very mixed feelings about their own childhood and in extreme cases act them out upon the baby. Thus they become over-controlling or under-controlling, lavish in their attention or depriving and/or abusive.

Keeping the environment safe Because the young child in an alcoholic household is completely dependent upon his/her parents, and survival depends on the availability of 'good parents', s/he must preserve the parents as 'good' no matter how bad or depriving they are in reality. In order to do this, the child attributes the badness to itself, perceiving that s/he must in some way be wrong or bad that his/her needs are not being met.

Inside the child's mind, two important transactions take place. Firstly, the bad aspects of the parents' behaviour (the deprivation and abuse) are owned as part of the child and these begin to attack and inhibit the healthy development of the child's mind. Secondly, as a response to this, the healthy growing part of the child's mind is submerged to prevent further damage or destruction.

This reorganisation of the mind and emotions has far reaching implications. The normal development of the child is arrested. The child loses contact with his/her thriving, growing part, often called the true or authentic self, and puts in its place a number of fronts or 'false selves' whose prime purpose is to protect the submerged parts from further damage, and to keep intact the parents as good, loving figures capable of ensuring the survival of the child.

Being bad to survive   In practice, this produces a number of paradoxes, for it means effectively that it is in the child's best interest to be as 'bad' as possible. For the more bad s/he becomes, either in anti-social, criminal, or plain bad behaviour, the more s/he is reassured that his/her parents are good and will be suitably nurturing.

Provoking abuse to survive   Abusive parents, either physically or sexually, are not complained about by their child, precisely because it is perceived to be the child's badness which has provoked the abuse from the 'good' parent. Indeed, it becomes desirable for the child to provoke further abuse given this disturbed perception of reality. Perhaps this explanation will help you to understand some of your own behaviour. Were you convinced of your own badness in this way? Perhaps you can now appreciate just why you find it so difficult to recognise when other people are being aggressive, and why you fail to stand your ground effectively.

Mummy's little helper   There is another side to this coin of adaptation and false selves. The child may take responsibility for the poor parenting by supporting and supplementing the parents' parenting. Children become mini-parents because they feel that it is their fault that things are not better. These situations can lead to incestuous relationships as the role of substitute parent is taken to its logical conclusion.

The bright capable achiever   A further adaptation that can take place, and perhaps you made this one, is that of achievement in academic or sporting arenas. This served the function of reassuring your parents that they must be all right, if they were raising such a bright and capable child. Although this might seem constructive, it can end tragically, if you begin to reach your limits and the achieving breaks down. Much more common, however, is the child who achieves more and more, but is still told that s/he is not good enough and must do better.

Neediness and shame   Because the real self is submerged, or more accurately, in hiding, the natural, healthy inclination to explore the world, and achieve a modicum of independence, becomes the subject of profound and all pervading shame. If this happened to you, you get a sense that there is something which is fundamentally flawed about you. This is a consequence of the reorganisation of your mind to preserve your parents as good. You have taken into yourself the bad bits of your parents which, inside you, begin to attack what you now identify as the seat of the problem – your own neediness. The rationalisation goes something like this: 'If I wasn't so needy in the first place, then my parents would not have the trouble they do in meeting my needs. Therefore, it is me who is bad to need and they who are long suffering to put up with me. What dedicated and good parents I have!' Of course, you do not consciously think these thoughts, the reorganisation of the mind is carried out unconsciously. Thus shame is felt in the presence of any needy experience, the need is denied, and feelings are frozen out of existence.

Imported aggression, that is, some of the bad aspects of the parents, can be dealt with in part by aggressive and destructive behaviour; if you become 'naughty', you preserve the good parent image. But it is never enough, you can never cope with the reserves of normal, healthy aggression most growing youngsters feel. There is also the problem of all the anger and resentment which must be denied and repressed, should you from time to time glimpse the 'real' situation. You begin to feel massively shamed in the presence of your own aggression and become self-destructive, self-punitive, and self-judgemental. Any aggression is wrong and further evidence of your badness and shame.

To understand how pervasive shame can be let us return to Michael, the man who could not play with his children, about a year after he began twice weekly psychotherapy with me.

Michael's continuing story

For several weeks Michael had talked about his experience of growing up in the shadow of his father's alcoholism. His mother, herself the child of a rather abusive alcoholic father, had spent much of her adult life in bed – suffering from severe migraines. She married Michael's father because he was 'so unlike her own father'.

Michael's earliest childhood memories are of doing errands for his mother, making sure that she was all right and not having to get up too often. He also looked after his younger brothers and sister, becoming a surrogate parent. He never thought his situation odd. He thought other children lived in exactly the same way. Friends, family, and neighbours would remark on how grown up he was and how well he helped his sick mother. He was not sexually or physically abused by his father, who was 'a nice man who would do anything for anyone, a real mate to all his friends in the pub'. It was, he told me, a normal, happy family.

As the therapy progressed, Michael began to get in touch with his anger towards his absent father and to grieve for his lost time with him. We realised that Michael's inability to play with his own children was connected to his wish to punish them because they were a painful reminder of the child within him who had never been played with. He began to feel a little better and was able to play with his children in a joyful and happy way. However, things were still far from all right with him, and we both realised that there were other deep-seated problems.

Some weeks later he became very depressed, following an argument with his wife. She thought that he should discontinue therapy as it was upsetting and preoccupying him, which in turn affected their sex life. We soon worked out that he was experiencing his wife in the same way as he had experienced his mother. He was not allowed to have needy feelings. Instead, his role was to help her and look after her needs.

I suggested that depriving his wife of sex was his way of avenging himself against his mother, who had so exploited him and had deprived him of her attention. (His mother had also suffered from serious depression, as she tried hopelessly to change her husband's drinking behaviour and to avoid the realisation that she had married someone who was far more like her father than he was different from him.) Michael suddenly became frightened by these realisations and sobbed uncontrollably for some time.

He told me later that he had felt suddenly exposed and empty, as though I could see his very soul. I said that I understood his fear, and I thought he felt that I was shaming him for his anger towards his wife, in the same way that his mother had shamed him for his anger towards her. This interpretation brought him great relief.

'You know, the words that you just used are words that I could never allow myself to use: shame – anger – revenge, yet they exactly describe how I feel. My life has been a lie, you know. I've lied to you, to my wife, to everybody, and yet even as I say these words I'm aware that I don't really know what the difference is between a lie and the truth. I have so much hatred bottled up inside me. That's wrong, I know, yet I even feel that it's wrong to try and get rid of it. I suppose I'm saying I am just plain wrong.'

Michael was beginning to understand how deeply ingrained his shame was and how pervasive it had been. In time he began to grasp how much he had imported attitudes and behaviour from his mother and father. Once he had gained this insight he could begin to change those attitudes and act in more constructive ways.

Michael's negotiation of the Autonomy vs Doubt stage of development, had left him with a deeply ingrained sense of doubt and shame. He had never truly separated from his mother and father, who, in their alcoholism and depression, had failed to offer him any effective mirroring of confidence in himself. His self-esteem was poor and his identity diffuse. The 'adult' Michael had not yet reached his second birthday, in terms of emotional growth.

3: Initiative vs guilt

This stage of development covers the period between three and six years of age, during which you need to progress from simple self-control to an ability to initiate activities and carry them out. You should also become far more involved with brothers and sisters and friends than hitherto. A favourable outcome to this stage is that you gain a sense of purpose and direction and can initiate your own activities. Parental attitudes still have a very powerful effect and if you are discouraged or they are dismissive of your achievements, then this can emphasise feelings of inadequacy, shame and guilt. Guilt should be clearly distinguished from shame. Guilt is experienced in the face of an action which is felt to be wrong or bad, shame is experienced when the individual feels that s/he is wrong or bad. Guilt can be rectified by reparation, shame cannot.

Parental consistency is vital during this phase. Guilt is the likely outcome, not if parents are overly restrictive but rather if they are inconsistent in their treatment of their child, who now begins to look up to his/her parents and imitate what s/he sees. It is at this point that role models first become important for children.

Alcoholic families also create difficulties if you are naturally curious, and ask awkward questions like 'why?' every few minutes. Yet this very much characterises children in this stage. Your questions might well be hushed up or ignored, and you begin to feel guilt: what did I do wrong? Let us look at the case of Jenny, a 53-year-old woman who requested treatment for her alcoholism.

Jenny, a mother in despair

Jenny came to see me six months after entering recovery from her alcoholism. She had reached 'rock bottom' with her drinking when her 19-year-old son attempted suicide, following a failed first year at university. Jenny was filled with guilt about her son's action and went to AA (Alcoholics Anonymous) meetings to conquer her drinking problem. Her son had since resumed his university studies but Jenny's intense feelings of guilt were threatening to spoil her new found and fragile sobriety.

'What's the point of living' she would say, 'if living means starting each day with self-criticism and ending each day with more self-recrimination? My sobriety, like my mothering, like everything else I do in my life, seems doomed to failure.' Within three weeks of first seeing me she had resumed drinking.

I told Jenny that I thought her resuming drinking was her way of taking charge of the therapy and destroying it, because nobody had ever before supported her in initiating and sustaining any project in all her life. I said that I thought she was very angry with me, and could not see how I, or AA, or anybody could be interested enough in her, or why we would want to support her. Her initial motivation to get sober was really guilt about her mothering, but this was not sufficient to sustain her in long-term recovery. Jenny insisted that it was I who had spoiled her recovery and made her feel bad. How could she trust anyone who accused her of being a bad mother.

Jenny ended her therapy, but wrote to me some months later. She told me that she had stopped drinking again and was attending AA. She wanted to apologise for her behaviour, and tell me in writing more about her life history. She enclosed a cheque to cover four sessions, and asked that I spend this time with her written work.

I understood that Jenny had to complete her therapy in her way: if I meant what I had said about supporting her in recovering, in her own individual way, then I would have to accede to her request, and not insist, as I might normally do, that she attend face to face therapy.

Jenny's mother was an alcoholic. Her drinking would start each Friday afternoon at 2 pm, and continue until Monday morning at 2 am. She would not drink, except for the occasional slip, outside these times. Jenny's father, too, was an alcoholic. Both parents drank over the weekend and he drank every weekday lunchtime and evening. Her father worked in the City of London, and the family was materially comfortable. Jenny had one sister, Ann, two years her senior. Their family friends were all 'boozy', and the family home was generally known as the place to go at weekends for a 'jolly good time'.

Jenny and Ann were very close and provided for one

another what little consistency there was in their lives. Nannies came and went, and the two little girls were relieved to go to boarding school when Ann was seven and Jenny was five. This gave them their first real experience of order and routine, although they both found discipline hard to take and initially both were 'difficult' pupils. Jenny continued along that course and was expelled at 14 for being drunk, smoking cigarettes, and having a boy in her dormitory. However, Ann went on to distinguish herself, was accepted into Oxbridge, and gained a first class honours degree in philosophy.

Jenny was sent to a boarding school for 'difficult children', and left at 17 with no formal qualifications. She then took a succession of jobs, mostly with 'friends of Daddy' in the city. She never stuck at any of them, but enjoyed 'the good life', drinking and partying. Jenny was very pretty, so there was a succession of boyfriends, until she met Roger when she was 21. He was an 'up and coming' executive, also fond of the good life and madly in love with her.

They married and had two boys, who were both bright and became high academic achievers. Jenny delighted in this. She would tell them, 'Where I could not go, there you shall go, doing it for me.'

Jenny's drinking escalated when her boys went to boarding school at 11 years of age, and her first dry days in over 30 years followed on from the attempted suicide of one of them.

We will return to Jenny's therapy later, but for the moment, let us consider the effect of her parents' drinking before she went to boarding school at just five years of age.

Monday and Tuesday were the worse days. Her mother was hung over and irritable, and Jenny would play quietly with Ann. By mid-week, mother was more approachable and would even spend time playing with her children, but by Friday morning she became preoccupied again, and was best avoided. Even so, Friday evening was the best time for Jenny. Her father, whom she had not seen all week, was home and everyone was in a jolly mood. Saturdays and Sundays were variable. Sometimes they were full of laughter and fun; at other times, Jenny and Ann kept well out of the way as there were furious rows. Saturday nights could be particularly frightening. There was a succession of party guests who would sometimes wander into their bedroom and turn on the light. Ann and Jenny would scream and mostly they would go away, but sometimes they would stay and want to talk to the children. One man once sat on Jenny's bed and patted her on the bottom, over the bed-clothes.

Jenny experienced her parenting as very variable. Her mother's moods dictated how she was treated and her playful activities were often cut short. In the end Jenny was left with a constant sense of guilt and doubt in her own abilities. She never really learned to initiate a project and follow it through to its conclusion. In her adult life she was beset with a pervading guilt and self-abasement, caused by vicious inner voices which constantly attacked her and spoiled her attempts to be creative or see her initiatives through. Her father's absence and her mother's variability did not support this developmental step.

It is interesting, too, that Jenny – in early adulthood – followed in her parents' footsteps, partying and drinking. It is in this third developmental stage that children first become aware of parents as role models, and Jenny certainly followed in the footsteps of her mother and father.

4: Industry vs inferiority

In this stage, which lasts from the sixth year through to puberty, you learn the skills valued by society. These include not only reading and writing, but physical skills and the ability to share responsibility and get along with other people. Your social world includes the school, neighbours, and extended family. The key issue during this phase is industry vs inferiority. In this context, 'industry' means that you feel useful in accordance with your growing ability to explore and achieve. A successful outcome to this stage leaves you assured as to your competence in intellectual, social, and physical skills. An unsuccessful negotiation will leave you under-confident, with a pervading sense of inferiority.

Inferiority and the alcoholic home   Although development in this stage is more crucially affected by the school environment than the home, the alcoholic home can make its contribution. Many alcoholics suffer from a massive inferiority complex, most usually disguised by grandiosity, false pride, verbosity, and an over-inflated ego. An alcoholic of this type tends to see room for only one 'genius' in the family, himself. The child who brings home her work to show proudly to an alcoholic parent may be rebuffed as the parent's jealousy and envy of her talent takes over, or, the parent may take credit for the achievement and exclaim how well he has done to produce a child with such talent. Either way, the child does not receive affirmation of her talents and accomplishments in a way that she can use to build self-confidence and competence.

Think, too, of how Jenny reacted to her sons' achievements: 'Where I could not go, there you shall go, doing it for me.' Jenny was enjoying a vicarious satisfaction in their achievements. Can you imagine the impact this message had on them? Is Jenny delighting in their achievement or her own chances of putting right something which had gone wrong for her?

A further way in which the alcoholic home can instil a sense of inferiority was described by one of our Scottish teenagers in Chapter 1. Morag's parents did not attend the school's open evening to see their daughter's art work, because of her father's drinking and the row between her parents. In such situations, the parents' absence, through their preoccupation with themselves and the drinking, becomes depriving and neglectful of their daughter's need for affirmation. It becomes difficult for the child to value her own talents and accomplishments when they seem of so little significance to the parents.

5: Identity vs confusion

This developmental stage covers the period of adolescence, and is difficult at the best of times because we are not children any longer, nor are we accepted as adults. Our task is to find direction and a set of values by which we can live. If we achieve a good outcome we will enter early adulthood with an integrated image of ourselves as unique. A bad outcome will leave us confused about who we are, where we are going, and what we want. We will be tied slavishly to our parent's values or will be living in reaction to them, but with no real sense of who we are or what we want.

Parents, for their part, have a seemingly impossible task. If they are too close to the young person then they hamper the separation which must take place, yet if they are too distant they will be accused of neglect and abandonment. They must provide a firm boundary and clear expectations about acceptable behaviour, while tolerating rebellion and dissension. Parents must allow young people to make their own mistakes, yet make sure that no irreparable damage is done.

The peer group is vitally important to the adolescent; acceptance or rejection becomes the major preoccupation.

We have already read some graphic descriptions of what it is like to live as an adolescent in an alcoholic household, as provided by the Scottish teenagers in Chapter 1. We can see how peer relations are affected because of the adolescent's acute sensitivity to being seen to be different or part of an 'out' group. The adolescent desperately wants acceptance and a feeling of belonging and shame at belonging to a family with a 'drunk in it' is exemplified by Fred's sensitivity to his schoolmates' snubs because he suspects they know about his father. His concern borders on paranoia, showing us the extreme sensitivity adolescents have about their acceptability. Let us now look at some examples of adolescent life.

Teenage years are when we become fully exposed to the adult world. We will become involved in sexual contact varying from kissing and cuddling to the loss of our virginity, and possibly living with someone, or married. As adolescents we will experiment with drugs of various kinds, including alcohol and tobacco, and possibly a substance such as cannabis; some of us will have experimented with heroin, cocaine, speed, and hallucinogenics. Music, clothes and fashion are also important as we become concerned to be up-to-date and impress our friends.

Sex Adolescence is crucially a time when young people become sexually aware. Physical maturational processes have occurred and young people have the obvious outward signs of their sexual identity. A girl will begin to menstruate, and need information about her body and reassurance that she is OK. The capacity to give this reassurance in the alcoholic family may be variable, according to the capacity of parents to distract themselves from their drinking. The young person's identity as a woman or man is now being formed and yet this may be 'missed' by his/her parents.

Drugs Drugs of all kinds pose greater than average dangers for children of alcoholics. They run four times the normal risk of developing alcoholism, so it is especially important for them to be aware of the risks they take when they consume alcohol and other drugs. Daughters of alcoholic fathers, by the time they reached their late teens, usually show different drinking patterns from other teenage women.[12] They have a larger average daily consumption of alcohol and drink more on separate occasions than their peers. They also have more drink-related problems and are more likely to use drinking as a coping method when faced with personal problems. A connection has also been demonstrated between parental alcoholism and bulimia in teenage daughters.[13]

Significantly more children of alcoholics had tried marijuana, and were also more likely to have tried hashish, speed and cocaine than other youngsters.[14]

There is also evidence of a connection between adolescent suicide and parental alcoholism,[15] which may make us think of Jenny and her son, whose attempted suicide prompted his mother to stop drinking.

Music and fashion Music and dressing like their peers are hugely important interests for the teenager. One observation I have made through my work at St Joseph's Centre for Addiction, is how teenage daughters can be copied in their dress by alcoholic mothers. It seems as though the mother abdicates her maternal role and begins to dress and act as a teenager. She may buy identical or complementary outfits to her daughter or borrow her daughter's clothes. Usually, the daughter will find this behaviour intrusive – and embarrassing. But it would be unrealistic to expect mother to 'act her age' before she has savoured the teenage 'fun' she missed out on long ago, bizarre though she may seem.

Emotional and social development   As we have seen, each one of us in the course of our lifetime moves through a succession of developmental stages.[11] As our bodies and minds develop, we become able to relate to ourselves and to others with increasing sophistication. Many things affect our emotional and social development and the quality of relationships in our adult lives depends on how we experienced our parents and other important figures in our childhood. If our basic childhood experience of our relationship with our parents was one of anxiety and fear, then we are likely to approach adult relationships with similar feelings and expectations.

The good news is that not all children from alcoholic backgrounds end up with major problems. Schools, neighbours, nannies, friends and relatives may all help to compensate for the parents' problems. On the other hand, poverty, homelessness (imagine living in a bed and breakfast hotel, with a single alcoholic mother), racism and other childhood traumas such as early death of a parent (a greater likelihood than in most homes) or divorcing parents may well compound the problems of alcoholism. It raises an important question which we shall turn to now. Why is it that some children appear to develop and mature *despite* their parents' alcoholism while others, often in the same family, are more profoundly affected?

Resiliance and risk factors

If you are an ACA, can you think of events in your childhood which seem to have been important factors in how you coped with parental alcoholism? Think about your siblings and how their lives have turned out. Who in your family has had the greatest difficulties and who seems to have been barely affected? Research suggests a number of key factors for you to consider in regard to your own situation:[14, 16, 17]

How old were you when the drinking in your family was at its height? If you were under six, you are more likely to have been seriously affected.

Sons, and particularly eldest sons, have been shown to suffer more; youngest daughters also seem to have more problems than older ones.

It seems that having an alcoholic mother is more damaging than having an alcoholic father.

Children with what is called an 'affectionate temperament' in infancy seem less affected in later life.

Children who are of above average ability suffer fewer problems in adulthood.

Each of these factors is based on statistical analyses of data and, of course, you – the reader – are not a statistic, so your own analysis of your family is likely to tell you more about risk and resilience factors for you.

The concept of resilience is a complex one. Some children by nature seem more equipped to cope with adversity; they are the born survivors. Others seem highly skilled at getting parents to look after them better, or maximising their use of the care that is provided. Others become adept at attracting and developing close relations with surrogate parents or caretakers. Therefore, when we talk about resilience we are not talking simply about an inborn or inherent trait of a child.

From my own clinical practice I have observed that if children think they know the reason why a parent is drinking, even if they are wrong, then this seems to increase their resilience. 'My Mummy is drinking because she is very sad', may be better than the self-blaming, anxiety and fear associated with having no idea or rationalisation for the drinking.

Children who have been sexually and physically abused, or have witnessed it, are more damaged than those who have not. They engage in more self-destructive behaviour, have more eating disorders and addictive/compulsive problems in adulthood, and are far more difficult to treat in a psychotherapeutic encounter than where the abuse was emotional.

Children who began abusing alcohol or other drugs in their early teens usually have far less ability to recover from active addiction than those who took up such habits later in life.

Further research

There is no area which I believe would benefit more from research in our study of alcoholism and the family than the identification of risk factors and resilience factors in children.

In the next chapter we shall move away from childhood developmental problems and back into the family as a system and the way in which communication is managed.

CHAPTER 3

Roots and Wings

SALVADOR MINUCHIN, a pioneering family therapist, working in Argentina, once described what he believed each family should provide for its children in order for them to leave their families with the best chances of survival and the capacity to thrive in the world. He suggested that the family should provide 'roots and wings' for their children or, in other words, a sense of belonging and an equal sense of separateness.

In this chapter we shall look at the alcoholic family as a system, the roles that it assigns to its members and how these roles are carried over into adult life, thus affecting the quality of life and the capacity to achieve fulfilment. It tells us about the context in which the individual characteristics of adult children of alcoholics develop. As we shall see, these characteristics are, in fact, a function of the family system and an attempt to maintain stability within that sick system.

Let me introduce here a concept known as homeostasis. This simply means that a change in the functioning of any one family member will lead to a compensatory change in another family member. For example, if my car breaks down on the way home from work and I cannot bath my children, which is one function I serve in my family, then my wife will have to bath them, compensating for my absence and acting as a 'homeostatic agent'.

We can liken the family system to an infant's mobile, in which a movement or shift in one figure on the mobile is compensated for by a movement or a shift in another figure, to maintain a balance. It is this shifting and adaptation in response to movement elsewhere in the system which this chapter seeks to describe.

I shall be emphasising the roles children fill in the family which most people would not recognise as causing difficulties later in life. In fact, when we see them in children, we often admire them. For example, many children of alcoholics can be so accommodating, eager to please, and self-sacrificing, that we might say of them, 'I wish I had a child like that,' or 'He is so good to his sick mother, it's great that he is so grown up.'

It has been estimated that about 40 – 50% of all children of alcoholics are of the disruptive, troublesome sort. We have already examined many of their characteristics in the previous chapter, because troublesome children come to the attention of schools, police, and psychiatrists, even if the connection is not made between parental drinking and their problems. We shall look briefly at the roles played by the disruptive and rebellious ones but here we shall concentrate on the less vocal and less obvious sufferers, that is, the over accommodating, pleasing children, for they may comprise the majority of children of alcoholics.

If you are the child of an alcoholic, and are so very nice and accommodating to others, it will explain some of the reasons why you can feel so empty, and lost. In some ways, you have the more difficult task, because as an adult none of your friends or even your spouse can comprehend why such a talented, lovely person, can have so little sense of self-value and feel so worthless and empty. They have been taken in by your role, and do not really know you.

This chapter offers you a chance to learn a little more about yourself and how you came to be the person you are. In particular, the role of shame, introduced in the last chapter, needs to be taken a little further because shame plays a very important function not only in individual development but in how the family contains the alcoholism, its denial, and the very effective 'happy family' front which many alcoholic families portray. Such families can be described as shame-based family systems because of the central importance of shame.

The man with a guilty secret

Let me tell you about an incident which occurred some time ago, as I was walking up the driveway to St Joseph's Centre for Addiction, because it gives an illustration of how shame can be expressed – sometimes in what may seem to you to be a rather odd or even extreme manner.

I met a recently arrived patient, an alcoholic – who was also the child of an alcoholic – hot-footing it away down the driveway in an obviously anxious state. I asked what had happened and where he was going. He told me that he had been in the middle of a lecture on stress when he began to feel uncomfortable and had to get away. I asked where he was heading for and he said that he was going to buy a 'deodorant' at the chemists. Surprised, I asked him how he was settling in generally at the Centre, and he told me that he found the therapy group he attended difficult. People were sharing difficult emotions there and he did not know if he could see himself as being like them; especially, he did not know if he was an alcoholic or not, or even whether he should be in treatment or not.

I said that they were important questions, and that I was intrigued that he was heading to a chemist to get a deodorant. I wondered if the deodorant was connected to his wish to protect the community from what he considered to be nasty odious feelings inside him. Did he perhaps fear that inside himself there were nasty smelly things which might leak out and if others witnessed this they would reject him? Getting a deodorant might be his way of masking the things about him which he felt were unacceptable to others.

With my encouragement, he returned to the Centre to talk to one of the counsellors, and disclosed that he had not been entirely honest at his admission interview. He had not told us that he had fathered a girl with whom he has little contact and about whom he was feeling upset inside. Only when such 'dark secrets' are out in the open can a patient begin to relax his guard and really benefit from the course of treatment – whatever form that may take.

The impulse to run away or to cover up, the need to hide or disguise, arises because we feel that if that which is unacceptable is exposed it will lead to rejection or abandonment by others.

It is also a feeling which arises from a comparison of oneself with others, in which one feels inferior. The chap in our vignette does not experience the inferiority because he denies the comparison in the first place – when he asserts that he doubts his likeness to other alcoholics and his need for treatment. A more common experience of shame leads to the characteristic bowing of the head and avoidance of eye contact due to an acute awareness of 'inferiority'.

Experiencing shame

Shame can be deceptive because it is not always experienced directly as a feeling. If we are deeply ashamed, then we defend ourselves by denying it and splitting it off from awareness. With the chap who was going to buy a deodorant, it reached consciousness as a fear about a bodily function – worry about creating an unpleasant body odour. Thus the body became the focus of attention rather than the emotion.

Shame and shattered expectations Shame is likely whenever our most basic expectations of a significant other are suddenly exposed as wrong. In a family with a drinking alcoholic this is a very frequent experience. Think of how Michael (Chapter 2) reacted when his father shouted at him. He froze to the spot. Children in such circumstances can feel devastated and shamed.

When Michael's father realised that his behaviour was frightening to his son, he tried to make amends and to comfort him. This was potentially a healing moment because his father's reaching out was intended to connect what therapists call the 'interpersonal bridge' between two people, in this case that he might comfort his son. But when Michael's father took the money and went to the pub, he lost the opportunity to re-establish that interpersonal bridge which had been broken by his sudden anger. Children often respond to the breach of the interpersonal bridge by becoming stiff and defiant, or unfeeling.

Shame and suddenness of exposure The suddenness of exposure is very important. Shame can be followed by extreme and intense rage – the horror film *Carrie* is a powerful study of shame, in which a teenage girl summons up and then unleashes a terrible, psychic vengeance on her peers for humiliating/shaming her by pouring a vat of pigs' blood over her just when she is at the height of pride, having been crowned the belle of the ball at the school graduation dance. This is followed by a murderous rage unleashed at her shaming mother who had punished her for her emerging sexuality at the point of her first menstrual period.

Shame and sexuality The link between shame and sexuality is also very strong, with the body and genitals typically being the object of the shame. (In the German language the genital region is called *die sham*, the pubic mound is called *die shamberg*, and pubic hair is called *shamhaar*.)

What do you remember about the way bodies and genitals were discussed in your family? Whether you come from an alcoholic background or not, my guess is that the majority of families in our culture communicate shameful attitudes to bodies and sexuality. For example, we tend to use euphemisms for sexual organs – we don't have a penis but rather a 'willie' – as though to use a proper name is in itself a problem. No wonder so many adults experience difficulties with their sexuality when, from the cradle, we are surrounded by so much shame about sex. How many families do you know who affirm children for gaining pleasure from their bodies? How many are prepared to discuss masturbation, wet dreams, etc? Mostly we leave it up to schools or vaguely hope that our children will find out sooner or later.

In alcoholic households, the situation can be more difficult because either parents do not talk at all about sex, or children are exposed to lewd comments or witness attempts at copulation by drunken parents. In either case the youngsters are left to make sense of it without guidance or information. Shame is an impotence-making experience because it feels as though there is no way to remedy the matter. One has totally failed as a human being.

Shame is healthy   Finally, it is important to understand that shame can be a healthy part of development, and functions in a positive way to enhance and preserve the sense of self, if it is displayed appropriately and sensitively. Children of alcoholics suffer from so much shame because they have been subjected to so much 'shameless' behaviour. The extreme self-centredness of the alcoholic parent means that he can never admit to being in the wrong.

Healthy shame brings us into an awareness of when we behave in ways that fall below our ethical and moral standards, especially in relationships. It leads us to humility and a realisation of our human fallability, and is a vital pathway to our inner self. Without this awareness we can not grow emotionally or spiritually.

Shame-based family systems

Understanding shame in its many guises is an important precursor to a discussion of a shame-based family system, because shamefulness can not only come to characterise children of alcoholics in their experience of neediness or aggression, but also the way that relations are managed within the family system.

In a healthy functional family   consistent behaviour and communication leads to the establishment of what is called a rule or belief system. For example, in my own family we believe in eating the evening meal together. There is no radio or television on, no books or newspapers are read, and any telephone caller is asked politely to ring back later or we agree to return the call. The children are expected to remain at the table until everybody has finished their meal.

Our belief system around mealtimes is that it is a good thing that we eat together and spend this time as a family. Although we do not adhere rigidly to the rules, for example, we don't get together every evening, and sometimes the children leave the table before everybody has finished their meal, we have dinner together often enough and the children stay at the table long enough for us to sustain our belief. There is a circularity between our behaviour and our beliefs. The more we eat together the stronger our belief becomes in the importance of this time together and the more we believe in our time together the more we make the effort to eat together as often as we can, and for the children to stay at the table for as long as they can.

In any dysfunctional family there is a loss of the circularity between the belief system and the behaviour. For example, the family keeps its belief system that it is important to have a meal together, but rarely does anybody turn up at mealtime, or if they do nobody talks, the television is on in one corner, and the newspaper is being read by someone else, and the children come back and forth to the table.

Faced with this contradiction a healthy family will either change its beliefs about mealtimes, or change its behaviour to accord with its beliefs. A dysfunctional family does neither. It holds on to its beliefs in the face of contradictory behaviour. Many children of alcoholics describe obviously depriving and abusive incidents from childhood only to add, 'We were, of course, a normal happy family.' Alcoholic families seem as addicted to playing happy families as the alcoholic is to alcohol.

But the happy family illusion is not bought without heavy cost to the emotional and social functioning of the family. It becomes isolated from social contact with the outside world. Children do not bring their friends home for fear that the presence of the alcoholic would be shaming. The non-drinking spouse withdraws from social occasions to avoid being embarrassed in public. In the absence of such contacts the family preserves the illusion, at least to the outside world, that they are a happy family.

Don't talk, don't feel, don't trust   Communication within the family must be stifled in order to maintain the illusion. Unwritten rules keep communication rigid. Family members do not talk about anything which draws attention to the alcoholism, they deny or ignore strong feelings, and the huge variability in behaviour – including many disappointments – destroys trust.

This rule system relies on shaming almost exclusively for its maintenance. If a family member were to talk about the problem to the drinker, the latter would attribute the problem to the complainant or to some other outside factor. The complainant eventually feels that she has got the wrong end of the stick and that there must be something wrong with her for having had the thought or feeling in the first place.

The alcoholic might become impatient or angry if the topic is broached again, he may even become threatening or abusive. In fear, the subject is dropped and the complainant concludes that if she does not talk about things or get upset, then things might be better. Eventually, she feels shame if despite her efforts she still feels angry or upset at alcoholic behaviour. In defeat, she might well withdraw into herself, becoming committed to the illusion.

If problems were discussed in an open and honest way, then the drinker would have to be confronted with the effects of his behaviour, and change wou.ᵈ have to be considered. But so long as the family remains in denial, illusion and shame, the drinking continues, and the happy family facade is maintained in the face of overwhelming contradictory evidence. No wonder children of alcoholics so often question their own perceptions and sanity. Perhaps you have felt this in *your* family, and may even have wondered if you were going mad.

Family tension and role playing

Living in such an unhealthy family environment invariably leads to tremendous stress, strain and tension. The family as a system must adapt itself to the insanity it is living,[1] and find ways of counterbalancing the effects of the drinking parent's behaviour. It does so by prescribing certain rigid roles for family members to play.[2]

The chief enabler The term 'enabler' is used to mean enabling continuing addiction. The chief enabler tends to be the spouse of the alcoholic. It used to be that the enabler role was thought of in a derogatory way because it could be quite clear to a neutral observer that the spouse, despite protestations that they wanted a drinking partner to stop drinking, would often behave in a way that encouraged continued drinking. They would pay debts, clear up messes, and tell lies to protect the spouse from the consequences of the drinking.

From the description of the reactive phase of the family illness of alcoholism presented in Chapter 1, it is clear that the whole family is affected by alcoholism. Alcoholic denial is a very powerful force, and it is not surprising that the spouse can become as deluded as the alcoholic. We now also know that many of those who marry an alcoholic are not coming afresh to addictions. They may well be children of alcoholics or other such dysfunctional families, and be reliving what seems 'normal' to them. The enabling role is important to the stability of the alcoholic family because it allows the illusion that the family illness is being combatted, when, in fact, it is being reinforced.

The martyr The martyr is also quite often the spouse, although not always. She may frequently berate and shame the alcoholic over his drinking, blaming his habit for all the misfortune which has befallen the family. She becomes extremely emotional and appears to be in great pain and hurt. However, the martyr is typically the most resistant to help. Secretly, she feels superior to the alcoholic and this superiority masks poor self-esteem and a strong sense of inferiority.

Martyrs do not want anything to change, because it would mean having to take responsibility for their behaviour and feelings without blaming them on anyone else. A martyr is likely to make confidants of quite young children and endeavour to get them on her 'side'. This poses problems for the children, who may be quite distressed by being put in such a position, but it allows the family system to continue in dysfunction.

The scapegoat   The scapegoat is the troublesome child who misbehaves in order to draw attention to him or herself and give the family something to focus upon besides the alcoholic. Such children often act out in noisy and public ways their need to be bad to keep their parents 'good', and in this way to maintain family stability.

The hero   The family hero is the one who brings great credit to the family by success in the world, thus feeding the illusion that things are not that bad and so no change is required. Jenny's son who tried to commit suicide is a typical hero. His academic achieving meant so much to the family, or so he believed, that he tried to kill himself because he failed some exams. His suicidal act was the key to bringing about change in the family. Jenny stopped drinking and made her first attempt at recovery. When roles are discarded the illusion can be shattered. Alternatively, the family may redouble its defensive efforts and become even more rigid and dysfunctional.

The mascot   The mascot is very much like the clown in the circus, bringing light relief, and rarely taken seriously. He or she can be quite genuinely funny and be important in diffusing tension. Mascots can be practical jokers.

The lost child   The lost child, like the mascot, is not taken seriously. He or she fades into the background and does everything possible to avoid conflict. Parents will often believe that the lost child is unaffected by their rows, or tensions in the family, because he is often in a state of withdrawal and appears preoccupied with private thoughts. In taking this role the lost child avoids getting caught in the crossfire and avoids being blamed for any problems, but he can be the most seriously damaged because of a characteristic tendency to internalise the pain of the family and brood upon it. Consequently, the family does not have to change or make adjustments to the lost child.

The responsible one   This is the role adopted most often by an only child or the eldest child in an alcoholic family. He or she takes responsibility not only for his or herself but also for sisters and brothers, and parents, providing structure for all in an often inconsistent home setting. Michael, the man who could not play with his children, is a typical 'responsible one'. His earliest memories, you may recall, were of doing errands for his mother, looking after younger children, and taking parental responsibilities. Such a role has obvious advantages for parents, and there is no impetus for them to change.

The adjuster   Adjusters are the typical 'easy going' children who seem infinitely flexible and able to fit into the most difficult of situations. They are extremely malleable, demand very little of the parents and seem 'happy' to go along with whatever the parents say or do, often with a cheery grin that masks true unhappiness. The adjuster has long since learned that it is pointless to make a fuss or be needy, and has long ago buried the pain of not having effective mirroring from either parent. Survival is best achieved by 'fitting in' and causing no fuss, feelings are effectively frozen.

Like 'the responsible one', he or she is deprived of an appropriate childhood, but in a different way. Adjusters show flexibility and endure stress which most healthy adults would have difficulty coping with. Of course, adjusters are only pretending; they are not coping or assimilating change at all, merely cut off from feelings and surviving by causing as little fuss as possible.

The placater   This child greatly needs to smooth over conflicts. He or she is very sociable and excels at making others feel comfortable and cared for. However, he is motivated by guilt that he caused the alcoholism, or might cause the family to split up, unless he smoothes things over for everybody. In this way, the placater helps the parents not to have to take responsibility for the marital relationship. He acts as balm between the parents, and may act as go between or comforter, if there are rows or disagreements.

Where do you fit in?

The roles examined above are not exhaustive. We could probably define over 100 separate roles that might be adopted in alcoholic families. If you are the child of an alcoholic you might be able to think of additional roles you or other members of your family played. Think of times of crisis in your family, what was your predominant feeling?

If your feeling was one of inadequacy and guilt, you are likely to have been a hero. If your predominant feeling was one of hurt and anger then perhaps you were a scapegoat. Lost children probably mostly felt lonely, and mascots felt fear. The roles may have shifted around between members of the family. The family hero may have changed into a lost child at some point or vice versa.

What was your experience? How did others behave? Even if you are not the child of an alcoholic, what was your family like at times of crisis? Does this help you to understand what it is like to live in a chronic state of crisis and tension?

All families are dysfunctional to some extent. There are no perfectly functional families. The best that any family can hope for is that it is good enough and that the burden placed on children to adapt to their parents' problems is not so great as to cause developmental impairment. There is conflict and cover-up in every family. If you read this and think to yourself, 'not in mine', then you are experiencing denial. Your denial may well bring you into the rather unreal world described here if it becomes excessive. You, too, might rely on shaming to prevent the truth from coming out.

Healthy families develop good communication channels and a capacity to resolve conflict and contradictions. Healthy families are places not only with a capacity for joy and happiness but also for suffering and sadness. In alcoholic families, suffering in children is anathema because the parents see it as an affront to their image. In healthy families, parents can suffer alongside their children and support them in their pain.

In many alcoholic families, consuming alcohol was an attempt to bear suffering. Sorrows were drowned there and pain numbed. Alcohol was invited into the home as a guest but over time came to be the master. Like matches in the hands of children, alcohol has burnt the house down and we can only believe the danger after the fact, as we walk about dazed, in the ruins of our family life, shocked at the devastation caused, and uncomprehending as to how such a thing could happen from such innocent play. Yet this is how we treat alcohol in our society. We do not place any warning on it to alert us to the dangers, and we fail to intervene to reach those most at risk, the children of alcoholics.

The disease of the disease

Alcoholism has been described as a man on fire running into the sea to put the fire out but drowning instead.[3] The shame base of the alcoholic family is the disease of the disease, meaning that excessive shaming so affects family communication that the disease of alcoholism is doubly protected. Shaming and denial are like the proverbial 'belt and braces' of alcoholism. If one should fail, then the other is sure to work to preserve the alcoholic from the realisation of the connection between his addiction and its consequences, the ultimate goal of any alcoholic and his family.

Multi-generational aspects

A family may take years to become shame based or it may even take more than one generation. I believe that all chemical dependencies and other compulsive behaviours arise from shame-based systems, as do many phobias and some depressive illnesses.

At St Joseph's Centre for Addiction, all patients complete a detailed family history, and it can be quite surprising to patients to realise quite how their family has been afflicted by alcoholism or other compulsive disorders in previous generations. Such information is helpful to the alcoholic entering recovery because he can appreciate the context in which his alcoholism has arisen and be aware of the difficulties his children might face.

Many spouses of alcoholics come from similar dysfunctional families. They may well have grown up in abusive or depriving families and 'choose' alcoholic partners because this is what seems normal to them. But it is often not a freely arrived at choice, rather children of alcoholics may well be driven by inner destructive forces, described in the previous chapter, to continue the family legacy and repeat again in a new generation the old patterns. They may also be in retreat from normal healthy relationships because they have not acquired the necessary skills.

There are further, more complex, ways that the intergenerational aspect displays itself in alcoholic families.

Inversion of the parent – child relationship

John Bowlby is a British psychiatrist who has carried out important studies of the interaction of parents and children. He understands well the dilemmas faced by children of alcoholics, and suggests that the request the child is responding to in the parent is as follows. Unknown to herself, mother (or father) is seeking belated satisfaction of a desire for the loving care she either never received as a child or perhaps lost. At the heart of this situation is an infantile part of the parent, which elicits a protective attitude from the child.

Bowlby suggests that the child performs two important functions for the parents. Firstly, he or she must reassure the infantile part of the parent that it will not be deserted or abandoned; this means that the child must not become independent and leave home. Secondly, he must acknowledge the 'good' parenting he is receiving by continuing to be dependent and needy. In this situation the parent's own anxiety about separation is ameliorated, and if the child eventually does leave home he leaves with a degree of guilt and misgiving which may bind him psychologically to 'home' forever.

According to Bowlby,[4] the parent concerned is 'inverting the normal parent – child relationship by requiring the child to be the parent figure and adopting the role of child herself . . . As a rule the inversion is camouflaged.'

Parental roles

Ellen Moorehouse,[5] an expert on alcoholic families, proposes four parental functions necessary to a child's healthy growth and development:

1: Role stability

A child needs to feel a consistent ongoing emotional relationship with the parents, and a consistent emotional reaction among any other family members. Although in healthy famlies roles may change, for example, the wife may return to work after having children, there is a period of readjustment followed by a further period of stability.

In alcoholic families there is role confusion: where a mother is the alcoholic a daughter may from time to time take the place of the alcoholic wife and be cast as the confidant and love-object of the father. And in more general ways, a wife with an alcoholic husband may set the stage for the rest of the family to relate to father as an authority figure when sober, and as one of the children when drunk, thus setting up role confusion.

2: Environmental consistency

This means offering a home that is safe and secure. In alcoholic homes, this consistency is often lacking. Families living in the midst of parental alcoholism are chaotic and unmanageable. It might not be clear, for example, who is sleeping with whom. Perhaps the parents sleep together when things are improving, then there is a relapse, and the non-drinking spouse may sleep with one of the children. If there is fighting, more of the children might want to sleep in the parental bed. Bedtimes for the children might become variable depending on which parent is looking after them, and their state of mind.

3: Dependability

This entails parents doing what they say they will do. In alcoholic families, there is a great impairment of parental dependability. In more functional families, there will be occasional disappointments and some let downs, a trip to the cinema might have to be cancelled at the last minute because of illness, or there might simply not be enough money to go on a holiday that was planned and looked forward to. In alcoholic families such disappointments occur with great regularity. Blackouts, in particular, can cause lack of dependability as the drinking parent simply can't remember promises made.

4: Emotional availability

It is crucial to every child that their parent is 'there' for them emotionally. The crucial ingredients to emotional availability are undivided attention for at least some of the time, being truly empathic, truly giving, or truly self-denying.

When the alcoholic is drinking, the child's needs are often ignored or alternatively indulged. In states of intoxication, the drinker is likely to be in a self-centred withdrawal. If he passes out he is completely unavailable. Even when sober, he may be irritable or alternatively smitten with guilt about his drinking and desperately trying to make amends to the child.

This chapter has illuminated some of the communication problems in alcoholic families, how shame and denial dovetail to become guardians of the addiction, and how roles are created to maintain the stability of the family. It is now time to look at children of alcoholics in adulthood – and as individuals.

CHAPTER 4

Adult Children
of Alcoholics

ADULT children are adults in their physical and social
functioning, that is, in that they have the mature body
and responsibilities of adults, and they will have a job, be
husbands or wives, and parents to children. But emotionally
they are still children themselves, in the sense that they
have not yet successfully negotiated their earlier developmental crises.

As we have seen, adult children – because of the way
their family has functioned – were really child adults in
their early years, coping with demands and roles which
fully mature adults might have found difficult or impossible.
Adult children are children who had to become 'adults' in
their childhood, only to find themselves confronted by their
suppressed childhood needs when they are grown up.

Adults children face some of life's cruellest ironies. Having
shown great courage and imagination to survive childhood,
adulthood offers few rewards and, emotionally, the adult
child continues to operate in survival mode.

It is a bit like a soldier who fights a war against a tyranny,
only to discover when the war is over that he is no more free
than he was before the struggle began. He has become like
the tyranny he fought, brutalised by the fighting and now
a replica of the very thing he most despised.

Adult children are all about hypocrisy. The term hypocrite
comes from the Greek word 'to be an actor', and adult
children are supreme actors in that they act and imitate
life itself but their 'real' persona is hidden in a protective
shell, having little or no part in the drama. Playing a role

has become second nature and many adult children do it to perfection. Only in mid-life are they likely to reflect on their achievements and realise that they are worth nothing and mean nothing. Inside is the gaping hole where the centre of the self used to be. It is as empty, lost, and hungry as it ever has been despite the food, drugs, sex, 'relationships'. If the adult child, does not go in search of the lost self and restore it to its central position and begin to grow again, he or she remains in denial and stays lost.

In this chapter we shall look at the characteristics of adult children of alcoholics (ACAs), find out more about the progress of Michael and Jenny, and meet other adult children of alcoholics. This will help you to appreciate that you are not alone. Many adult children share common characteristics. It is unlikely that you will identify with every characteristic described, but you will see yourself in many of them.

For those of you who question the extent to which you are affected by growing up in an alcoholic family, this chapter will prove very illuminating.

Characteristics of ACAs

Janet Woititz, a pioneer in the children of alcoholics field in the USA, produced a list of thirteen characteristics of ACAs.[1] In this book they serve as thirteen headings under which I have broadened and deepened her illuminating descriptions to take account of my own experience of working with people in the UK.

1: ACAs guess at what normal behaviour is

ACAs guess at what 'normal' is without realising that there is no one normality. There are a whole variety of different norms which individuals, families, and societies live out. Because ACAs have grown up in an environment that has instability, variability, and survival as the norm, their perceptions are distorted.

As a child you may have avoided inviting people into your home but you may well have spent long periods of time in the homes of others. In these other homes, you will have been treated well as a guest, possibly fed well and, if your friend's family was aware of some of the problems in your home, they may have given you special, sympathetic treatment. This may have left you with the mistaken impression that this was the norm for that family. You did not realise that families may be on their best behaviour when guests are around; family conflicts may have been hidden in your presence. Even on a very basic level, the family you visited may only have had ice cream for dessert when guests were about – and not every day. Thus your view of a normal family was not – and still may not be – very realistic.

Even where young children of alcoholics do not visit other homes, they are known to look in the windows of neighbours' houses and guess at what wonderful homes are within.

Children of alcholics seem more likely than most to use television and film to inform their ideas of normality. Whereas the ordinary adult might find a programme like *The Waltons* sugary and idealistic, many ACAs become transfixed by the loving, caring, warmth displayed there. The ACA will compare his or her life with what s/he sees on the screen and feel disappointed and jealous that s/he can't have what others have. Perhaps you have felt like that.

In adulthood, it can be difficult for you to grasp that a normal healthy family life has conflict and difficulty, and that the norm you aspire to is really an ideal that you are highly unlikely to reach. Being the adult child of an alcoholic you are likely to see this as further evidence of your inadequacy. For example, Michael, the man who could not play with his children, watched his adult friends play with their children, made comparisons and found himself lacking. He did not realise that his friends did not always play well with their children, until he had been in therapy for some time. I asked him to observe more closely their play and to enquire what it was like around bedtime, when the children were tired and before mealtimes when they were hungry. He found that many fathers grit their teeth at such times, or even avoid their children. This was an enormous relief to Michael, who had always seen such times as evidence of his own inadequacy. He was shocked to find out that some fathers got angry with their children and that this was OK.

Michael never had a father who could safely be angry with him, so how could he know that this is a normal response to children when they are being difficult? Michael's selective perceptions of his friends' relationships with their children, and his idealised role models, had not encouraged Michael to be a father. All the 'shoulds' and 'should nots' filled his mind and inhibited him from showing the love he felt for his own children.

I am sure that you, the ACA reading this book, can think of other examples of guessing what normal is. You may have been playing roles all your life, but it is very hard to stop because you are frightened that you will be 'found out', that everyone will discover how little you know, what a shameful creature you really are. Your pretending and guessing actually reflect the best that any young child can manage if they are bereft of good role models. How were you supposed to know how to do things or what is appropriate now? Your parents were preoccupied and you were left to work it out yourself. You did the best you could but maybe it is time to move on now and start to do things differently. As you will see later, there is a way out.

2: *ACAs have difficulty in seeing a project through*

Many ACAs can think of instances when they did not complete a project or course of action that, at one point, they felt so passionate about – from decorating a room to finishing a doctorate thesis. Money is wasted, time is wasted and, although there is always a good excuse (or lie) to rescue you from complete embarrassment, 'I was ill,' or 'They did not recognise my talent,' and so on, the truth is that very few if any projects have been completed, ever. So why should this be such a prominent feature of ACAs?

- First, alcoholic parents are notoriously inconsistent. If they say they will do something it does not follow at all that they will. There are so many broken promises, so many times when planned events do not happen or are are aborted. Of course, there are always good excuses or even if there are no excuses proffered the real reason is never discussed: that daddy's drinking comes first.

- Secondly, few ACAs have memories of parents who could problem solve effectively. Even practical tasks like mending broken items in the house were rarely, if ever completed. If a fence had to be mended, it would always be done 'soon' or 'next week'. The truth is that the fence was never mended, or a temporary slipshod job was done, amid much ceremony and protest. It is also a feature of many alcoholics that they will do work for neighbours or friends but take a very different attitude to their own family and home. It is easy to play 'the good chap' role with those who only know you in a superficial way, rather than with your family, who know you fully. Problems at home may always have seemed overwhelming, and the skills needed to break them down into smaller, manageable steps were never demonstrated. Team work may also have been absent, so there was no sense of a parental couple or a family doing things together.

- Thirdly, it is likely that no one sat down with you, when you were younger, and worked alongside you, showing you how to plan and complete tasks. Parents may have had high expectation, but no real support was given. They did not know how to get close to you and help you. It is no surprise that ACAs should be characterised as having difficulty in seeing a project through.

Jenny, the alcoholic ACA who sought my help after the suicide attempt by her son, is a classic example. She completed very little in her life. She was expelled from school, she took no exams, could not hold on to a job, and did not complete her first attempt at psychotherapy.

Many ACAs can learn to turn this trait to their advantage, as Neil did.

The story of Neil

Neil is a very successful songwriter and some of his songs have been No. 1 hits. He is 36 years old and is a recovering heroin addict. He came to London over two years ago to kick his habit; at the time his heroin use was costing him in excess of £100 per day. Two of his friends had died through drug abuse. Neil had seen enough.

With the help of a friend he locked himself away for two weeks and went 'cold turkey', attempting sudden, unassisted withdrawal from his drugs. He was frightened to return home, where he knew he would be pressured to take drugs again. Instead, he rented a flat in London, told his friends that he was going to work in America, and planned to live incognito for a year, concentrating on his recovery. He shaved off his hair and his beard and contacted me for help, having heard about me through a friend who consulted me briefly.

Neil refused to enter a residential drug treatment centre; he said this was for fear that he might be weakened in his resolve if he was surrounded by other drug users. When he became more able to accept responsibility for his behaviour and feelings, he admitted that he was also frightened that he would not be able to stay the course.

Neil was a very frightened man when his drugs were no longer available to him. He came to see me twice weekly for 14 months and worked extremely hard at his therapy. There were two periods of three weeks each when we met five times a week, in addition to daily telephone contact, as Neil began to experience again the traumatic loss of his father when he was two years old. He needed to know in a very concrete way that I would not desert him. I persuaded him to attend Narcotics Anonymous meetings, in addition to his therapy, as he would find support and encouragement there from people who were further along the path of recovery from drug addiction than he.

I knew that Neil would get no support from his family. His mother is an alcoholic and after the sudden death of her husband the rather precarious control she exercised over her drinking deserted her and she plunged into incessant drinking. So Neil effectively lost both parents.

We shall return later to Neil's story, but at this point I would just like to draw attention to an aspect of his professional life which is interesting because it is typical of many ACAs to put a deficit of character to good use. Neil was originally a singer/songwriter, but rarely managed to sing in public. Early in his career, he would develop sore throats on the night of a 'gig', or he would be late, or become so frightened of performing that he would just not show up. Understandably, his opportunities dried up. Luckily, however, his talent was immense and he was persuaded to concentrate on his song writing. In this way Neil snatched success from his failure to complete his project. Although he would dearly have loved to sing his own songs, and could not, his musical talent did not go to waste.

3: *ACAs lie when it would be easier to tell the truth*

Lying is endemic to alcoholic family systems, whether it is the excessive use of denial of painful realities or the very obvious lies that family members engage in to cover up the alcoholism. For example, those of you who are ACAs, how often did you hear the non-drinking parent ring someone up and say 'my husband/wife is unwell and won't be in today'? And how often did *you* lie to protect the drinker in the family from discovery, or simply to make life less unpleasant for yourself? Lying for a purpose eventually becomes gratuitous lying. The purpose is lost but the behaviour continues.

Michael, who could not play with his children, lied to me on several occasions when telling the truth would have been easier. Once he rang me to cancel a session with the excuse that he would be working away from London that day.

The real reason he could not come was because his work partner was out of London and Michael could not leave the job he was working on *in* London. There was no real point to the lie, he could have told the truth and it would have been perfectly acceptable. Instead, the lie became his guilty secret.

On other occasions Michael was 'economical with the truth'. At one point he told me that his wife was questioning his continuing in therapy because of the cost involved. What Michael did not tell me until later was that he had spent the previous three weeks moaning about the recession in the building trade, and suggesting he might go bankrupt. The truth was that he was winding his wife up to worry about money so that he could feel justified in leaving therapy and blame it on her, and the recession. He found the therapy painful and hard but, although he was aware of a wish to run away and we discussed this, he continued to be economical with the truth. Michael needed the guilty secret as a barrier to further closeness to me.

Neil, the songwriter, constructed a charade of lies around his decision to quit heroin. He did not have to tell his using friends lies about giving up heroin, and nobody really believed that he was going to America anyway. The lying was more part of a way of life. He told fantastic stories to get attention, because he believed that if he did not dramatise his life then he would not be interesting enough.

He still could not understand why his mother deserted him when he was two years old, he was aware only of feeling so frightened and shocked. At some point he surmised that if he could draw more attention to himself and dramatise his life then he would not be ignored. Of course, paradoxically he could not perform to a real live appreciative audience, because his songs were not lies; they came from his heart and were passionate and moving, the very qualities which he believed would lead to his rejection.

ACAs often report the experience of becoming aware of lying halfway through a sentence. They wish to say 'stop, let me start that again', but they don't to avoid embarrassment.

ACAs can also become masters of what are called post-hoc rationalisations. If, for instance, they behave in an impulsive way and do something which with highsight seems stupid, such as buying shares just as the market is about to fall, they may well claim that the shares were bought after long and careful consideration, as a long-term investment. They may claim to have anticipated the short-term fall in value but this did not deter them in making long-term decisions. Lo and behold, some months later the shares are resold at a profit and turn out to have been a sound investment, or so their friends might think. Only the ACAs know the truth – that they were lucky and did not really know why they bought the shares at all, except that it seemed a good idea at the time and that their poor impulse control overwhelmed them.

Some ACAs discovered in childhood that their parents preferred lies to the truth. 'How are you today?' may be a parent's question. If the truth is given in reply, 'Not so well. Actually, I'm struggling a bit today,' the parent may have become critical or attacking: 'If you listened more to me you would not feel that way,' or 'Well pull yourself together and stop moaning.' The child learns that it is easier to say 'I'm OK.' It means a lot less hassle. In this way, children learn not just to lie about events but also about their feelings and experiences.

4: ACAs judge themselves without mercy

In the section on emotional development of COAs we saw the reorganisation of the mind that the child must accomplish to maintain an image of the parents as being good, because such a perception is vital to the survival chances of the child. The bad characteristics of the parents were taken into the child and once internalised begin to attack the vital growing parts of the child's mind and send them into hiding. In adulthood, it is this attacking part of the mind which stands in judgement and assaults from within. It contains the 'should' and 'should not' messages, topped up with shame and guilt.

ACAs also often judge themselves not against fallible

human ideals but rather against highly idealised characters. Can you imagine how it would feel every time your family fell below the standards of loving care promoted in *The Waltons*? You would not feel very good about yourself. And, of course, it would be all your fault, because a bad person like you is bound to cause trouble for others and deserves to be deprived and punished.

5: *ACAs have difficulty having fun*

It is not difficult to understand why ACAs don't have fun – they are too busy exercising self-control and overcoming impulsiveness. Having fun means 'letting go' and as an ACA you dare not do this because you can never really be sure what might come out. Good healthy 'letting go' is not modelled by alcoholic parents. Using drugs and alcohol is the way they overcome inhibitions. It is the chemicals which are responsible for the letting go, not the person.

In some families, as in Jenny's, there was a good deal of fun and laughter in the home, but it could never be trusted not to turn into something nasty and dangerous. This fearfulness inhibits the fun times and makes children of alcoholics over-controlling and cautious. In Jenny's case, although she appeared to be a fun-loving partygoer in her late teens, she was more reckless and danger seeking than fun seeking.

She had sex with many men without taking precautions but did not become pregnant. She was very lucky not to have ended up in serious trouble through her 'fun'.

Having fun is also associated with being childish and ACAs interpret this as being a nuisance and an inconvenience, so it has very negative connotations. ACAs are often stiff and unresponsive around those who are having fun. They may not even get the joke, although they will laugh nervously so as not to stand out in the crowd.

6: *ACAs take themselves very seriously*

ACAs take themselves very seriously because from their earliest years they had to be mature and responsible, and relinquish childhood prematurely. One ACA I know very well has a photo of himself at 18 months of age, and a more serious face would be hard to imagine. He appears to have the troubles of the world on his shoulders and he had yet to say a comprehensible word of language.

ACAs can become the butt of jokes because of their seriousness. They are often thought of as prudes or killjoys because they lack the capacity to join in fun. Also, they can be excessively intellectual and pedantic, giving great thought to trivial matters.

Many turn to drugs or alcohol in an attempt to remedy their seriousness and to let go. And, as we now know, the ACA is at great risk of developing a serious drug or alcohol problem.

7: *ACAs have difficulty with intimate relationships*

This is the characteristic which needs least explaining, because the bulk of this book has explored the ways in which children of alcoholics are affected when a parent's drinking permeates almost every aspect of the family's functioning and, consequently, the child's relationships both within the family and outside of it.

8: *ACAs over-react to changes over which they have no control*

This is a direct consequence of growing up in a family in which changes and sudden disruptions of the environment were a common experience. If this was your experience, you may have tried to change your parents or the environment to gain the stability you required, but failed because you were powerless over the alcoholism. However, it did not stop you having strong feelings and reactions when events outside your control seemed to determine your survival. ACAs can appear rigid and uncompromising over what appear to others to be minor changes to a planned outing or event. It seems as though life itself might depend on a trivial matter.

Michael had several instances where he did not finish a piece of carpentry because the customer asked for changes in the design in the later stages of work. The changes were often minor but he would insist on carrying out the work as originally specified or he would walk out on the job. He could not bear to deviate from a course of action even if he could see the good sense in changing. This over-reaction to change over which he had no control is his continuing attempt to master the anxiety roused by sudden changes of mind or plan in his childhood environment.

9: *ACAs constantly seek approval and affirmation*

Groucho Marx summed up perfectly the very ambivalent attitude of ACAs to approval and affirmations, when he said, 'I would never belong to a club that would have me as a member.' ACAs constantly seek approval and affirmation, yet when they get it they denigrate it or reject it. Look at the following dialogue between an ACA and his lover.

ACA: 'Do you love me?'

Lover: 'Of course I do.'

ACA: 'But do you really love me?'

Lover: 'Yes, I told you I do.'

ACA: 'But do you really, really, love me?'

Lover: 'Look, I told you already, that I love you.'

ACA: 'But do you really mean it?'

Lover: 'Look, just leave me in peace, you're driving me mad.'

ACA: 'You see, I knew you were angry with me and that you don't love me.'

Lover: 'You are impossible sometimes, but I love you just the same.'

ACA: 'Are you sure?'

Lover: 'Good grief!'

This dialogue is typical of the ACA in his approval seeking. He desperately wants to be loved and approved of but he doesn't know what to do with love and approval when he gets them.

There are several good reasons why this might be. In alcoholic families words are cheap. Because someone says something doesn't mean very much, unless they are being critical; then this makes a great deal of sense and is accepted without a problem. It is compliments and affirmations that cause difficulty.

In alcoholic families there are many double messages. The most common one is 'I love you – go away.' At one moment you are given full attention but then, as the alcohol takes effect, the parent becomes self-preoccupied and rejecting. You become confused and wonder what you have done to deserve the good treatment and what you have done to deserve the rejection. Of course, it is not your actions which have caused the parental behaviour but you do not know that. In adulthood, when you hear 'I love you', you are waiting for the second half of the injunction: 'go away', and as in the dialogue above you bring this very situation about, eliciting a rejecting response by persisting with the question.

10: ACAs usually feel they are different from other people

The Scottish teenagers in the first chapter illustrated how parental alcoholism made them feel apart from their friends.

Remember Fred's acute sensitivity about whether his school mates knew that his dad was a drunk? Teenagers from alcoholic homes know that their family is different and this knowledge sets them apart. They miss out on important adolescent experiences so that in adulthood they still feel they are apart and different. How different this would be if the same stigma was not attached to alcoholism. If the teenage ACA could realise that up to five million others in the UK are similarly afflicted by this terrible disease, then the social isolation might be ended.

In the reactive phase of alcoholism, family members isolate themselves even within the family, to avoid contact with the alcoholic or the rowing parents, so even at home the child feels apart and unsupported. This tendency to isolate is also carried over into adult relationships. Furthermore, because the ACA takes himself so seriously and doesn't like fun that much, he may well find friends hard to come by.

Another characteristic of some ACAs is their tendency to live life as a victim, perceiving themselves as being at the mercy of others and with little power or ability to take responsibility for themselves. Although in childhood this may have been an accurate reflection of their position, in adulthood it may set them apart from others, because each victim is only complete if there is a victimiser to play opposite. This is not a popular role for others to play, so there are relatively few volunteers for the position, unless an alcoholic or some other self-absorbed person can be found to fill the vacancy. In this way, children of alcoholics may marry an alcoholic and the cycle is repeated in yet another generation.

11: ACAs are super-responsible or super-irresponsible

This characteristic is common among ACAs. You may have an ACA working for you who is always on time, always working long hours without extra pay, anticipating your every need and smoothing your path. S/he can be relied upon in a crisis, can offer good firm leadership in your absence, and is the ideal personal assistant. I must admit to some ambivalence about the continuing recovery of such people who have worked for me as employees or junior colleagues. As their recovery progresses they become better at looking after themselves and are less self-sacrificing. They begin to say 'no' to unreasonable requests, and put me in a position where I have to take more responsibility for myself and my work! Although this is as it should be, it can take some adjusting to.

The super-irresponsible ones are those who have given up trying to please and are in full rebellion – anti-dependent. Their message to you is, 'I don't need you and I hate authority, so don't give me any advice or guidance, even if I ask for it, because I will only throw it back in your face.' They may also say implicitly, 'Don't depend on me, or I will let you down.' Super-irresponsible people are so obviously angry and unhappy. In childhood they tried desperately to please their parents but their efforts were ignored or deprecated. If they did well, they were criticised; if they didn't do well they were also criticised. They reckoned in the end that it was as well to be hung for a sheep as for a lamb.

In an employment situation the super-irresponsible may well rise to the top because they can be ruthless and give no thought to the feelings of those around them. Whereas the super-responsible may get to the top without trampling on too many others, and will be apologetic to those who *are* hurt, an irresponsible one, if s/he reaches the top, will have trampled on everyone possible and be surrounded by enemies. S/he will rule by fear and motivate by bribery, and may gain respect but never love or admiration.

The super-irresponsible who do not succeed become bitter and destructive. They undermine authority and corrupt vulnerable colleagues if they can. They may break the law, and if they are caught will regret only that. Those ACAs who become involved in criminal activity are likely to develop into hardened criminals because they are fully identified with their role of the 'bad one' in their family of origin, the role that was established to protect the alcoholic by providing a distraction from his drinking and its effects.

In adulthood, the role is carried on and it is hard to see alternative behaviours or to tolerate feelings of any sort, because any signs of weakness might be exploited by others. However, in recovery such people find enormous rewards for their changed lifestyle, and the risks are well worth it as the heavy burden of such a role is relinquished.

In some ACAs it can be very confusing, because they vary from one extreme of responsibility to irresponsibility. For long periods of time such people are super-responsible and self-sacrificing. They ignore signs of stress, become unwell and eventually burn out. At this point, massive reserves of anger and resentment well up inside and they become destructive and hugely irresponsible. They may steal or undermine the work of others, or let people down badly. They retreat into the victim role and may leave or be sacked. If they do not learn from their experience, and this may be impossible in the victim role, then they are likely to repeat the whole process over and over again.

12: ACAs are extremely loyal, even when the loyalty is clearly undeserved

Children of alcoholics have learned unquestioning loyalty from their earliest years. Their loyalty has been to a family system which protects the alcoholic at all costs. Is it any wonder that in adulthood they display unquestioning loyalty and commitment to people and systems undeserving of such loyalty? ACAs with this characteristic tend rarely to ask the question, 'what is in it for me?' Instead, they disbelieve contrary evidence, or make excuses for thoughtlessness.

Neil, the singer-songwriter, was mercilessly exploited by his first record company. He signed a contract which was patently unfair to him. As he found fame and earned more money, he employed a business consultant who told him he would stand a very good chance of successfully contesting the contract in court because it was so blatantly exploitative.

Neil could not bring himself to do this, despite the fact that he knew he was being taken for a ride, because he considered that he owed the company a debt of loyalty. In truth, his loyalty was connected to a wish to hold on to what he had at all costs and not repeat the disruption and loss of his early years. In time, Neil allowed his business adviser to negotiate his contracts so that his best interests could be protected.

13: *ACAs are impulsive. They tend to lock themselves into a course of action without serious consideration of alternative behaviours or possible consequences*

This impulsiveness leads to confusion, self-loathing, loss of control over the environment, and spending an excessive amount of energy cleaning up the mess.

It is said that ACAs have only two speeds in a lot of activities and relationships: full speed ahead, and full reverse throttle. Some ACAs want everything now, delayed gratification seems an alien concept. It is not difficult to understand why. If you have grown up in a family where promises are constantly broken and where you cannot rely on future events happening as planned, then if something is available now you might just grab it to make sure it does happen. Also, if you grow up with one or two parents who are impulsive in their behaviour it is hard to learn about impulse control because it has not been modelled for you.

Many ACAs report a sort of tunnel vision which justifies the full speed ahead description. Activities or relationships are entered into without any pause for an evaluation or re-evaluation. The ACA plunges in and, once committed to a course of action, cannot seem to stop. Very much like the alcoholic with his drinking, once one drink is consumed a compulsion takes over and attempts to control behaviour once the compulsion is active only make things worse.

In relationships many ACAs get deeply involved with people they hardly know, they neglect to get to know someone well before making a commitment. When disaster strikes this sort of ACA may move into full reverse, turning completely on its head the situation of only a few hours previous. They drift from one disastrous entanglement to another, learning little or nothing on the way. They begin to love the adrenalin highs of the drama.

It is not surprising that ACAs should also expend great energy in trying to clean up messes they create. They have grown up in a family system which prepares them perfectly for this job. For years they will have been around the mess created by the alcoholic and become conditioned to trying to smooth over the consequences.

This outline of the traits or characteristics of ACAs, although valuable in helping ACAs to identify how their adult character has been affected by childhood experiences, is really but a cross-sectional or snapshot view of life in adulthood. To understand adult children of alcoholics more comprehensively, in the next chapter we must return to where we left off in Chapter 2, and consider the remaining three developmental stages that follow on from adolescence.

CHAPTER 5

Out of the Frying Pan and into the Fire

MANY of you may believe that emotional and social development stops when we reach the age of 18 or 21 and our adult life begins. Nothing could be further from the truth. As we progress through adulthood there are three distinct stages of development: early adulthood, middle age, and old age. A successful outcome to each of these stages of development is vitally important to our continued wellbeing. In this chapter, we will look at development through these years and see how an alcoholic upbringing affects maturation.

Stage 6: Intimacy vs isolation – early adulthood

During the years between 20 and 35 the vast majority of ordinary adults commit themselves to an occupation or career and most will marry or form intimate relationships. Intimacy means an ability to care about others and to share experiences with them. Those who cannot commit themselves to a loving relationship because they fear being hurt or are unable to share, risk isolation. A successful outcome to this stage of development will be an ability to form close and lasting relationships and make career or work commitments. Many different sorts of relationships tend to be negotiated in these years, including sexual, platonic and working and/or collegial relationships. Competitive and co-operative relationships must also be established and conflicts resolved.

Many ACAs, having survived alcoholic families, enter early adulthood with a misplaced optimism. Perhaps this was your experience? You dreamed that as soon as you could get away from home and take life in your own hands then everything would be all right. You may have been bitterly disappointed to find that the compromises made in earlier stages of development have left you very unprepared for adult life and that once again you face a struggle for survival.

You may be suffering the effects of your codependency, that is, the adaptations you made to fit in with your alcoholic family, and will display some or many of the characteristics that have been outlined. You may even be finding yourself far more adapted to alcoholism than any other form of relationship.

Being an alcoholic, or living with an alcoholic, may be difficult and painful but at least it is 'normal' to ACAs, who often opt almost immediately for the path of alcoholism or marry an alcoholic. They enter adulthood ill equipped for the demands of intimate relationships, and so at the first setback they retreat into adolescent crises of identity and role confusion. In this way they avoid facing the Intimacy/Isolation crisis, and do not meet new and growth enhancing opportunities, the very lifeblood of potential recovery.

Adult children of alcoholics can end up in full retreat from intimate relationships as a reaction to a number of specific fears. Understanding what these are, and perhaps recognising some of them in yourself, will help you to avoid following this particular downward path.

Fear of losing control ACAs can be stifling to partners in intimate relationships. They try to control their environment and the people in that environment. Being in an intimate relationship with an ACA has been likened to being taken hostage. If you are involved with this type of ACA, you will know what this means. It can feel that you are constantly under surveillance, that your every mood, feeling, or action is of significance to your partner. The ACA may not recognise how controlling they are. They think they are showing loving concern.

The ACA may also experience sexual difficulties connected with the fear of losing control. Michael suffered from delayed ejaculation; Neil suffered from premature ejaculation, and Jenny rarely experienced an orgasm.

ACAs are also controlling because of the related fear of abandonment. Ironically, it is usually a combination of all these fears which drive partners away, and which lead the ACA into retreat from intimacy and back to something more familiar. ACAs also classically confuse love with pity. Partners will feel patronised and infantalised. The ACA feels puzzled that his or her loving care, as they perceive it, is being rejected. Thus the ACA in retreat will seek out someone with a serious problem such as alcoholism or a physical or mental illness, someone they can feel safe in pitying/loving. In this way, the ACA does not have to face the fear of abandonment or losing control.

Fear of feelings   Because of the shame experienced in the face of needy and aggressive feelings in childhood, many ACAs lose touch with all feelings. This does not make for healthy intimate relationships. If every time you have a feeling you flee from it and if every time your partner expresses a feeling you become uncomfortable, then you are a very difficult partner to have. ACAs may try to establish intellectual partnerships instead. A healthy partner is likely to be bemused at this and may give up on you, unless they understand why you behave in this way and you show a commitment to change.

Fear of conflict   Most ACAs are terrified of conflict to the point that if they see a fight or altercation in the street which has nothing to do with them they will feel guilty and frightened, as if it was their fault. This is not a good recipe for an intimate relationship in early adulthood. Relationships of any quality grow based on the capacity to handle conflict, not on the capacity to deny or flee from it because it is too frightening.

You may fear conflict because as a child you were

physically abused or witnessed parental violence towards a spouse or sibling. Witnessing a parent's anger getting out of control is very, very frightening to a young child because you genuinely fear for your own or someone else's life. You may have lain awake at night listening to the verbal fighting going on downstairs between parents, and felt deeply distressed. For these reasons you are over-whelmed by fear of conflict and avoid sorting out even minor altercations.

Coping strategies

For many ACAs the first ventures into intimate relationships lead to a retreat into less healthy relationships. Many ACAs become depressed and desperate, others develop addictions and compulsions, while some, mostly the hero types, sub-limate their intimacy needs through success and achievement in their career. Still others enter helping professions where they can channel their love and care in a structured, useful way. These categories are not mutually exclusive but we will look at each separately.

Depressed and desperate   It is tragic to see defeated and dejected young adults whose childhoods were tainted by alcoholism in the family, now facing a world where they just do not seem to be able to fit in. They describe themselves as voyeurs looking upon life, feeling excluded and on the outside. Unfortunately, many will be treated for mental illnesses which may further reinforce their feeling that they are faulty people: that there is something wrong with them. Nothing could be further from the truth.

If this is your situation, you are very much a casualty of alcoholism and your depression and despair are trans-formations of the impact on a normal person of living in an oppressive and damaging environment. Some may seem to be too far gone down the road of the mental patient role to be retrievable, or the damage seems too severe to be repaired. Life may seem lost to its great potential. But there is always hope if you are prepared to come to terms with your history and begin taking responsibility for your thoughts and feelings now.

Addictions and compulsions About half of all patients treated for alcoholism and drug addiction at St Joseph's Centre are children of alcoholics. Other treatment centres similarly report figures of between 40 – 60% as the average. Although many may not enter treatment until their middle adult years, the vast majority reach the early alcoholic phase before they are 30, and many will be in a state of addiction before they are 35. Other compulsions and addictions include compulsive over- or under-eating, compulsive gambling, sexual and relationship addictions, physical exercise addiction, and workaholism. (The heroes, and those who enter helping professions, are the most prone to workaholism.)

Heroes Family heroes (whom we first met in Chapter 3) tend to come into their own in early adulthood. By their mid-twenties many have become highly successful in their chosen careers. They may well marry simply because they think it is time they should, and have children because they aspire to the image of the happy family. Typically, if you are a hero, you spend little time at home and expect your husband/wife and children not to make demands upon you that would interfere with your career. You may well be divorced and remarried by the time you are 30. To the outsider, you appear to have it all: money, a smart car, and status.

In early adulthood heroes enjoy the thrill of competing and winning. Each success drives them on to greater effort. However, as time progresses, winning becomes boring, meaningless, and empty. An enormous emotional and spiritual crisis looms.

The helping professions Just as every boy who plays football as a youngster dreams of turning professional when he grows up, so the ACA relishes the prospect of putting to good use all the training and skills acquired in his/her alcoholic family. If this is your chosen path, whether you become a doctor, nurse, social worker, teacher, or psychologist, you will be carrying on the training and the encouragement you received as a youngster to care for the life and welfare of another person. From your earliest years you may have been a confidant to the non-drinking parent. You may even have been the marriage guidance counsellor to your own parents. You may have tended to the physical needs of a sick parent. So entering a helping profession seems a natural step.

Of course, not everyone who enters a helping profession does so because s/he is the child of an alcoholic, but it offers an avenue where ACAs and other codependents can put to good use skills learned in their dysfunctional families. It allows a sort of intimacy to develop between client/patient and professional which may be a substitute for more open, less defined relationships where there is a more equal balance of power and responsibility.

Working in helping professions also helps the ACA to manage intimate relationships. These professions usually demand long hours, for little pay, and crucially unsociable hours – perfect excuses for not mixing with contemporaries doing the ordinary social things that young adults do together. As a consequence, social opportunities are limited and the fears of the young adult about intimacy can be avoided, or experienced in more manageable ways. In addition, friends and relationships may well be made with others who entered the helping professions for similar reasons. Thus you will find people who are more like you and isolation is avoided.

On the down side, children of alcoholics are more prone to burn out than most because they fail to take notice of stress related problems and may continue to work beyond their capacities until illness or breakdown intervenes.

Those who find ways around the crisis of Intimacy/Isolation in early adulthood may feel that they have got one up on life at long last, that they have done well despite their difficult early years. But they may receive a nasty shock in midlife, where the problems which have been stored up from adolescence and young adulthood can come home to roost.

Stage 7: Generativity vs self-absorption – middle adulthood

Middle adulthood or midlife encompasses the years 35 – 60 approximately. For many people the years from 35 – 45 are particularly productive. It is peak time in most careers, if you are going to reach the top of the tree it will be during this period that you do so. Women who left the labour market in order to be with their children may now be thinking of returning to work or enjoying a less hectic home life and perhaps becoming involved in political or community groups or projects.

The crisis faced in midlife is generativity vs self-absorption, generativity meaning a concern with guiding and providing for the next generation. Satisfaction comes from a feeling that one's contribution to society is of value, helping one's own children through their teenage years, and perhaps adopting protégés at work who will look to you for wisdom and experience. The person in midlife may also become more politically and socially active as a means of being of value to others.

Self-absorption is the negative outcome of this crisis. You are left with depression and despair at a wasted life, the lack of contribution to your fellow man, and the lack of meaning in anything you have done. For many this becomes an impetus for radical change. For example, a man who has worked in the City may decide to sell up and move to the country, to grow vegetables. A woman 'happily married' for years may have an affair. The film *Shirley Valentine*, in which a woman refuses to return from a holiday in Greece to her boring, repetitive life is a classic example of the midlife crisis in action. I believe this film was enormously popular mainly because it touches a chord in all of us when we see someone break free from rigid, repetitive roles.

For most ACAs the midlife crisis is a painful time

because it becomes impossible to carry on in denial and avoidance. There are a number of ways in which ACAs are particularly vulnerable to problems in midlife. These include faulty grieving, a tendency to react rather than to act, a tendency to see life in black and white terms, and an over-developed sense of responsibility.

Faulty grieving The midlife crisis crucially involves a review of how life has been lived and how choices have been made thus far. For instance, a business career may have been chosen at the cost of a career in one of the professions, say in accountancy or law. The ACA in his early adult years may have congratulated himself on how much more money he was earning in business than his friend who became a lawyer. In midlife, he may begin to question his choice and experience regrets. Most people in this position will eventually come to terms with the choice they made. A sort of grieving for a loss occurs but then there may even be a renewal of a commitment to their chosen career.

The ACA may not find this process so easy. The capacity to grieve over even small losses involves calling up the memory of other, greater losses; ACAs typically have a huge backlog of losses which have not been adequately grieved for. The alcoholic family, living in denial, does not tolerate the emergence of strong feelings, and alcoholics usually have a huge backlog of unfinished grieving, because they have refused to acknowledge the painful realities which confronted them.

The ACA may well have a reaction to small losses in midlife that seems wildly out of proportion. They may enter a long period of depression which can only be remedied by professional help, for the ACA may well be faced with grieving for the loss of a whole childhood, and the 'happy family' myth. Such feelings can be overwhelming and may be too much to sort out without skilled assistance.

Reaction rather than action Many ACAs become hyper-vigilant, always on the alert for potential trouble, and they develop a knack of spotting trouble before it arrives. It is not difficult to see how useful this survival skill can be if you grow up in an environment where the behaviour of others is very unpredictable. In early adulthood you may well put this survival skill to good use in your career. You cope well with crises and are a cool head to have around when perhaps all others are losing theirs. You keep control and react to swift and unpredictable changes. For example, ACAs may well have ideal skills to deal in the stock market, or emergency work, such as in the fire, ambulance or police services.

In midlife, the tendency to react to crises may be less advantageous than the need to act upon the products of contemplation and review. You may see a need to change but not know how to go about implementing this. You may emotionally be back in your alcoholic family, waiting for the next crisis and feeling powerless to prevent it happening. You are far more 'at home' being in a position where you are powerless to change your environment, than creating an environment for yourself.

Seeing life in black and white ACAs with rigid, controlling personalities tend to see life in black and white. You may never have learned to tolerate ambivalence or ambiguity. Early in life, you became completely identified with your role. As you grow older you may begin to see that life is not so straightforward, good and bad or right and wrong are not so easy to distinguish.

A successful negotiation of midlife depends on a capacity to tolerate ambivalence and to consider the grey areas of life. ACAs can encounter enormous difficulties here and may well become depressed because of their inability to sort out these more subtle issues. For example, it is not uncommon for an ordinary person in adolescence to be a raving communist, in young adulthood to be a raving conservative, and by middle age to become more philosophical about politics. The ACA may find it difficult to become philosophical, for he or she has developed no way of coming to terms with the limitations of any political ideology.

Over-developed sense of responsibility   Many ACAs have an over-developed sense of responsibility. They worry very much about other people, and their self-esteem depends on their capacity to please others. They have a need to be perfect. At midlife, ordinary adults become concerned to pass on to their children and to society their knowledge and skills. At work they are aware of the new generation of up and coming young adults. Enormous pleasure is derived from 'adopting' one or more of them and training and honing their efforts and skills. It depends crucially on a capacity to sit back and cultivate others.

The ACA tends to get this aspect all wrong. Because of the overwhelming desire to please, they tend to take over others and control them. They find it very difficult to let others learn from their mistakes while supporting and encouraging them. As a result, they pass on very little of value and do not get the satisfaction that otherwise would have ensued.

Many ACAs find this developmental stage a depressing time. Those who developed a drinking problem in young adulthood may accelerate down the path of alcoholism.

Alcoholic ACAs   At St Joseph's Centre for addiction, the majority of alcoholic patients are aged 35 to 50. Their bodies are beginning to show the damage inflicted by years of excessive alcohol consumption. They may have liver problems or some other physical manifestation of alcoholic drinking. The ageing body can no longer stand up to the constant assault of alcoholic poisoning. Having been made physically ill they have no choice but to face up to the prospect of giving up alcohol. For the first time, perhaps, comes the realisation that they are killing themselves with alcohol. Thus motivation to stop drinking may emerge.

Mentally, the alcoholic in midlife may be able to see that his fundamental belief in self-control and exercising will power over alcohol consumption is flawed and he is able to glimpse that, try as he might, he is powerless over alcohol. He may become ready to ask for help.

Emotionally, he realises that he is empty and dejected,

becomes aware of the friends he has lost, the family he has damaged, and the suffering he has inflicted on himself and others. Guilt and shame replace arrogance and grandiosity. Fear of being alone and deserted in old age also becomes prominent. He may be filled with sadness at the wasted opportunities and damage caused by drinking.

Spiritually, he is bankrupt and broken. He is nobody and nowhere despite any material possessions he may have acquired. Relationships are empty and painful. He does not know his children, and his spouse may be estranged.

The ACA in treatment becomes painfully aware of how his alcoholic parent may have died alone or in complete self-absorption and will determine not to end up the same way.

The choice he faces is clear and unequivocal. He can continue drinking and follow the path to its logical conclusion, which is further damage and ultimately death, or stop drinking, and begin a new life with the potential for growth and development that sobriety brings. At St Joseph's Centre, I have witnessed many people who have made the courageous decision to stop drinking. I have also seen many who have been unable or unwilling to face a life without alcohol and I have felt sadness at the continuing mayhem. However, I respect their right to make such a choice and firmly believe that the role of the professional is to bring people to a place of choice but not to inflict change or bully them into health.

It is a fundamental human right to live life as we each see fit to live it, even if, as a result, such a life is unnecessarily blighted by an illness which we now know to be treatable. The alcoholic is ultimately accountable for his behaviour, even if he acts with diminished responsibility. As a society, we must determine how to protect children when the alcoholic acts with diminished responsibility towards them, because children have an equal right to our protection. I do not believe that pregnant, alcoholic women who continue to drink should be imprisoned as is the case in one state in the USA. This punitive action tends to be perpetrated on poorer sections of the population and may cause more damage than is prevented. At the same time, we should not turn a blind eye to the many babies born with birth defects caused by drug and alcohol abuse by their parents.

Stage 8: Integrity vs despair – old age

The final stage of development covers from 60 to death. The developmental crisis of integrity vs despair is concerned with the way one faces the end of life. Old age is a time for reflection. To the extent that one has successfully coped with the problems posed at earlier stages, one has a sense of wholeness and integrity. Death can be faced with a sense of fulfilment and satisfaction. If, on the other hand, life is seen as a series of missed or bungled opportunities and failures then the final years will be marked with despair. In such a frame of mind there may be bitter resentment of other people for not doing more, as external reasons are sought to account for the disappointment that life has been.

The way ACAs approach old age is crucially dependent upon the resolution of the midlife crisis. If the alcoholic ACA has found sobriety, then these years can be golden. Because so much of life has been wasted by active alcoholism, the ACA in recovery appreciates more than most the value of each new day in sobriety. If he is a member of Alcoholics Anonymous and following their programme of recovery, he will have made amends as best he can to those he has hurt through his drinking. If the family also finds recovery then there can be a celebration of recovery for all as they enter the family unity phase outlined in Chapter 1.

If the alcoholic does not find recovery, he may not reach this stage because his body will deteriorate and he may die prematurely due to the effects of alcohol. His children, now grown up, will face life as yet another generation of ACAs struggling to survive, and possibly finding recovery for themselves in their own right.

It seems to me that the greatest blessing is peace of mind. In old age, our sight and other senses may be fading and we may face illness or disability. This can be unbearable without peace of mind. This was brought home to me very strongly, some time ago when an elderly ACA wrote to me because she needed someone to whom she could tell her story. I went to visit her and was greatly encouraged by her belief that it is never too late to tell your story so that death can be faced with courage and peace of mind. The letter was written following an article in *The Guardian* newspaper by Liz Hodgkinson. I will end this chapter with the letter:

Dear Friend,

Since reading Liz Hodgkinson's article on Adult Children in *The Guardian*, I've been trying to make up my mind to write to ask you if you can help me. You see I am 89. Nearly every attribute in the article I seem to have suffered from. It seems that I am a half-person who never really grew up.

I don't intend to inflict my life story upon you, for I realise that I am too old to join a group – even if there were one up here. But I wondered whether you might have heard from one or two people around here who could perhaps help each other?

If I could only tell the whole miserable story in *absolute truth* to someone before I die, I might shed the load of guilt, lies, deception, etc, etc, and perhaps realise who I really am. I know that this should be a clergyman's job, but though I've known many and really liked a few I never felt I could really 'spill the beans' to any.

I don't think that I am especially senile, though I do forget the names of people and places. I still drive my old car, and possess over seventy years clean licence!

I am a widow, whose husband was a well loved doctor.

I do feel guilty for troubling you at my advanced age, but *The Guardian* article was an absolute eye-opener to me. So please forgive me. With many blessings upon you all at St Joseph's, and the wonderful work you are doing.

Yours sincerely

Stopping the Rot

RECOVERY simply means stopping the rot caused by the adaptations made in childhood to the dysfunction in the alcoholic family. Let's look at some of the principles of recovery that I have used successfully and what they mean in practical ways. These 14 principles are not exhaustive but rather reflect what I have learned about recovery in my own life and in the lives of those of whom I have had the privilege of knowing.

Many ACAs – perhaps yourself included – having read the previous chapters of this book may be feeling somewhat overwhelmed by the extent and pervasiveness of the effects of the behaviour of an alcoholic parent and the family system in which they lived in their formative years. It would be typical if you were to feel frightened and overwhelmed with the magnitude of it all, and to conclude that recovery is impossible for you. This is not the case. Your recovery can start at any point. The first principle of recovery that I am proposing is:

1: Recovery is for everyone who chooses it

Recovery is possible for everyone who seeks it in an honest and committed way, whatever the past damage.

Honesty here means that you will seek after recovery with your heart as well as your mind. Recovery is not an intellectual process, although you will have to apply your mind to it. If, on the other hand, your desire for recovery is heart-felt – and in this way honest – then a vital first step has already been taken.

Commitment means that you are willing to act to bring about change. You will not alter a thing unless you decide that it is desirable to do so. Many commitments that ACAs have made in the past have been made on impulse, and then the next day they have reverted back. The choices that it may be necessary to make will need to be carefully thought through in all their implications, and only then will you decide to go ahead. However, you must be aware of the natural human inclination to want to feel better but not to want to have to do anything differently in order to achieve the increase in good feeling. Being willing to change in order to improve your life is vital.

2: Your difficulties are the result of the adaptations you made to your alcoholic family. Your response was the act of a sane person living through the insanity of familial alcoholism. You can unlearn many of the things you learned in childhood and decide how you are going to behave

Many of the characteristics you acquired in growing up in your family were learned behaviours and strategies that ensured your survival. For example, your capacity to fade into the background in your family may have saved your life, or at the very least prevented further damage being inflicted upon you. Such adaptive behaviour was necessary then; it may not be necessary now. If you are lonely and friendless now, it is no good continuing to fade into the background; it simply does not work as a strategy for making friends.

Recovery is about identifying those learned behaviours and strategies which preserved survival and sanity in childhood but have become redundant to the changed circumstances in your adult life. This does not mean that you need to make dramatic changes overnight; the process can be slow and protracted. It might be wise to experiment with change in the first instance, before committing yourself to a course of action. You may even decide to retain some of these characteristics because they are so useful to you. For example, if you work in hotel management you will need to continue to be a 'people pleaser' in your working life, but you may decide to change this behaviour in your personal life, as you seek a more intimate contact with your partner and friends.

The purpose of recovery is to bring you to a point of *choosing*, not to replace one set of oppressive rules with another.

3: *The growing and loving part of your self can be retrieved from hiding and grow again in the present day*

The vital, growing, and loving part of yourself which became submerged for its own protection during childhood is just waiting to re-emerge, given half the chance. In fact, you will probably discover that it was not completely submerged in the first place. There was always a small part on the lookout for nourishment and encouragement, and hungry to absorb whatever was available. However, it will still be in a child-like state, and predominantly a state of fear and shame.

It may be helpful for you to think of this part of you as the 'child within'. Recovery is about locating the child within and involving the child more directly in your life. For example, if you make a big decision, such as to emigrate, you may begin to feel anxious and fearful. This is the child within telling you that you have not yet thought through all of the consequences of this decision. Alleviating the anxiety and fear by thinking through these feelings is what is meant by involving the child in your life. You may end up making the same decision, it is not the decision which is crucial to the child but rather that he or she is listened to and involved. The greatest threat to your recovery comes from denying and ignoring your child within.

The image of a child within has been found by many adult children of alcoholics to be a very powerful and important tool to aid recovery. It may help you to articulate and express feelings and experiences which otherwise would be negated as childish or selfish. If you have a childhood version of your name, or perhaps a nickname by which you called yourself, for example Gaz for Gary, then ask yourself what Gaz would think or feel about a situation or position you find yourself in. In this way you may begin to locate the child within and regain spontaneity and a greater sense of wholeness.

Locating the child within and drawing closer to him also has an important spiritual dimension. Jesus taught that we must become as children to enter the kingdom of heaven, and Krishna consciousness portrays God as a manifestation of childlikeness and youth.

4: The child within is likely to need healing of past hurts to be fully free to live in the present

The process of healing is a very natural one. It requires of us only that we bring about the right conditions for it to take place. In the same way that a broken leg heals if it is placed in a protective casing for a few weeks (that is, we do not have to heal the breach ourselves), wounds from childhood will heal if we can bring about the conditions in which healing can take place. Two conditions necessary for healing are: the presence and use of safe places and safe people.

A safe place is any place in which you can be still. By stillness I mean a state of mind in which you are able to listen to yourself and be open to the promptings of inner voices. A safe place might be your kitchen late in the evening, or it might be a church or museum. I live just a few hundred yards from the River Thames, and have discovered that simply sitting on the river bank and watching the water flow by is refreshing for me. When you have discovered one safe location, search out others so that you have more than one to go to. These are not places of distraction or avoidance but of retreat.

You may well discover that much of your leisure time is spent where there is distraction and amusement. There is nothing wrong with that – they have a role to play as well – but they are not safe in the sense that I have in mind. A safe location is one in which you can open up to thoughts and feelings of all sorts, not where such experiences are forgotten or avoided. Once you have found safe places it is important to spend time there.

The crucial ingredient in a safe person is that he or she is non-shaming – that is, a person who will not ridicule or attack you for having thoughts and feelings that he or she does not like. In time you will learn how to handle shaming people but in the early stages of recovery avoid close contact with them. A suitable person is non-judgmental in his or her attitude to you. You are accepted for who you are, warts and all. Such people are inoffensive to you. This does not mean wishy-washy or prudish but rather non-intrusive. Their views are not imposed on you but differences of opinion are accepted. Your right to make your own judgement is respected, even if you are wrong. A safe person is one who can tolerate anger and upset in you, without having to retaliate or reject you. When you have spent time with such a person you feel more alive and refreshed. The child within you feels acknowledged and nurtured.

There are many safe people in the world. Often, but not always, they are middle-aged or elderly, happy to impart their wisdom to the next generation. It is a healthy part of their development, to be a mentor, so you will help them as much as you help yourself. If you join a self-help group (see Chapter 7), you will be introduced to a system called 'sponsorship'. A sponsor is someone who you identify as being further along the path of recovery than you are. He or she will have grown in a way that you respect and you will aspire to 'have what he or she has'.

If you choose to follow an overtly spiritual path, then

God – however you define Him – will be a very safe person for you. The God of my understanding is constantly reaching out and making Himself available. He accepts people just the way they are. There are no conditions attached, except that you reach out and accept His hand. We shall return to overtly spiritual paths in Chapter 7.

Whoever you choose to be the safe people in your life, and wherever you choose as your safe places, the search itself will be enriching. In time, you may become a sponsor or mentor yourself, and feel the joy of giving away freely what you have fought so hard to gain. In the meanwhile, spend time with safe people and go regularly to your safe places; healing will follow at a safe pace.

5: *Recovery will cost you time and attention*

Recovery is not bought cheaply. There is no instant enlightenment nor are there any worthwhile shortcuts. It will require of you patience, discipline, contemplation, and balance.

Patience is perhaps the most difficult quality to develop. Like many ACAs, you may become discouraged very quickly if you do not see instant results. Recovery may be very slow and proceed in a stop-start fashion. There may be long periods spent consolidating gains made, and other times when you appear to be going backwards. Far from being evidence of regression these are important times. Don't forget that you can only proceed at the pace of the child within. The child may need to check things out to make sure they are real and substantial. The child is frightened and anxious about change. If you become intolerant and impatient it is a signal that nothing much has altered, and your child may retreat into hiding once more. It might also be that you are not able to handle further change until some sort of stability returns, despite your genuine desire to move forward. At such times you will need discipline.

Discipline means that you give attention to the structure in which change is taking place as well as to the changes themselves. For example, are you spending consistent times in safe places and with safe people? At times of discouragement and despair, discipline is important because you are going to continue to do things which will nurture recovery even though you can see no results and feel no motivation to continue. If you rely purely on the momentum of success in making obvious gains, then your recovery will be short lived, or you will seek after false highs and fool yourself that you are making progress when you are not.

Finding time in safe places in which you contemplate your position is important. Contemplate how your life was before you began your journey into recovery. Is it really preferable to return there? Remember, too, that a balanced life has its highs and lows, its joys and its disappointments. What is important is the thread of continuity that runs through all of these experiences, not the experiences themselves. Hold on to the thread which saw you through all the ups and downs of your childhood, and let go of the present disappointment or despair. This may well restore your balance.

6: Getting rid of things is more important than taking new things on board

Stopping the rot, you may be surprised to discover, will involve getting rid of things rather than taking new things on board. If you are feeling empty and lost in your life, it is far more likely to be because you are surrounded by clutter and debris than because you are in a desert-like environment. Taking anything new on board before you have discarded the clutter will only exacerbate your emptiness. Furthermore, ceasing to do certain things will be far more important than imposing further activities. Finding still places and safe people depends chiefly on letting go of many past activities. This will become self-evident as you progress.

7: *Recovery is about giving up trying*

Recovery will also mean trying a lot less hard or, in fact, giving up the act of trying altogether. Although your alcoholic parent may have tried as hard as he could to stop drinking and your whole family attempted as hard as they could to cope, these endeavours made no difference.

At this very moment, try to scratch your nose. What happened? You either scratched your nose or you did not. You *decided* to do it or you decided not to. *Trying* to scratch your nose is a way of not doing it; it is a recipe for failure. Living in an alcoholic family system has given you a very distorted idea about willpower. You will have tried to influence all sorts of things that were beyond your powers of influence, and nobody will have told you that you have human limitations in what you can change by an act of will.

You witnessed a whole family attempting to exert power over something that, in actual fact, they were powerless over, and you will have had little experience in being effective – applying yourself to things that will make a difference. There is a prayer that is used by many people in recovery to emphasise this point: God, grant me the serenity to accept the things I cannot change, the courage to change the things I can, and the wisdom to know the difference.

8: *Life is for living in the present*

A further surprise about recovery from codependency, that is, the adaptations made to the dysfunction in your family, is that it concerns itself far more with your present life than with your past life in your alcoholic family. You cannot go back and change a single thing that happened to you. The past is useful only as a learning resource to be applied to present living. Introspection is a present time activity. Even reliving past trauma in psychotherapy or some other safe environment is only useful in so far as it frees up necessary energy to be applied to living today.

Paradoxically, those who ignore the past and avoid the pain from that time, and by an act of will try to live in the present, are doomed to failure. They become hostages to their past and live crippled lives in the present: they have still not understood that their relationship to willpower is distorted, and they will continue to re-enact past traumas in the present and not learn from them. Learning to live in the present is important. You cannot recover yesterday and tomorrow may never come. You may well have learned this in your alcoholic family where 'tomorrow' or 'soon' really meant never.

9: You cannot recover by yourself

In your alcoholic family you survived by isolating yourself. You thought there was something wrong with you and you went into hiding. You have literally millions of ACA brothers and sisters who felt the same way. You will be surprised how much you have in common with them. Like the ugly duckling, you will eventually become a swan.

You can help other ACAs and they can help you. Your isolation was a survival tool to get you through your childhood. If you are to grow beyond mere survival, however, you will have to decide not to isolate yourself any longer. Whether this means joining a self-help group alongside other recovering ACAs or not is an important decision to make. If you decide not to have this contact, an alternative means of breaking your isolation will have to be found. Finding safe people to support you in your recovery is of the utmost importance.

10: You can't grow or learn unless you make mistakes

It is vital to make mistakes. This is not to suggest that you bounce from one disaster to the next but rather that you learn to make new mistakes. Codependents, before they find recovery, appear to make many mistakes. In fact, they are making the same mistakes over and over. In recovery, you become able to make new mistakes and to learn from them. There is so much that you do not know about yourself and relationships. You have lived a life that is narrow and impoverished of healthy role models and positive experiences.

Making mistakes and being able to admit to error has an important function in reducing shame. Humility and honesty are the enemies of false pride, grandiosity and arrogance. In your alcoholic family you may well have witnessed a parent, or parents, experiencing great difficulty in admitting being wrong. To be so might have seemed to them to be weak or to involve a loss of face. In recovery you become able to do what they could not do; you embrace the process of making mistakes as a friend, and you begin to learn, sometimes in hard and painful ways, how wrong you can be. In so doing you climb a learning curve and that particular mistake is not made again. Your life will be enriched by the experience and you will have grown a little more.

11: The more you find out about yourself and others the better

Recovery means being able to acknowledge how much you do not know, and being prepared to find out. Begin to read more about alcoholism and its effects, and, in particular, find out more about yourself and other people by asking for feedback, and articulating what inside of you have always felt like 'silly' questions. For example, in lovemaking be prepared to ask what your partner likes and what s/he does not like, and ask for what you like, or if you don't know, be prepared to find out. Don't assume that you know. Your sex education, like so many other important parts of your worldly education, may be very limited, not because you are stupid but because nobody in a responsible role ever told you.

Conversely, you may have been exposed to many experiences before you were mature enough to handle them and they have become laden with fear and anxiety. For example, if a recently bereaved friend becomes upset you may find yourself withdrawing – either literally or metaphorically leaving him/her alone. Be prepared to ask if s/he would like you to remain. S/he may wish to be held or comforted, s/he may not. Don't assume that you know when you don't. Be prepared to find out.

In your family, so many assumptions were made that served to protect the alcoholic in his drinking; adults were not taking responsibility for themselves. When your non-drinking parent became upset she may have turned to you for comfort. She may have complained about the drinking partner to you and you felt torn between your anger for the drinking parent and your love for him. Therefore, comforting someone became problematic. In recovery you become able to learn about things that you assumed you already knew – by asking more questions of yourself and others. Your exploration of the world has been limited, you have been holding back and avoiding so many things for long enough.

12: Experimenting is the best way of finding things out

New experiences do not come cheaply. You cannot learn anything unless you take risks. Initially, this means carrying out limited experiments.

For example, if you are prone to overwork, find out what happens if you take one day off, stay at home and do nothing. Do not arrange to see anyone or fill up the day with any activity. Don't even turn on the television or read a newspaper or book, if you can bear to be so inactive. Avoid alcohol, tobacco, or any mind-altering drug. Get sufficient food in prior to the day so that you don't have to go shopping, and cook the food beforehand so that you don't even have to cook on the day itself. Get nice food in, a treat if you can afford it. Listen to the voice inside you that might tell you that you don't deserve such nice food, but don't act upon it. Buy the nice food.

If you are married or have children, tell them what you are doing and ask them to co-operate. If they think you have gone mad or ridicule your experiment, listen to them and explain again that this experiment is important to you, and stick to your plan whatever they might think. If you are a parent with small children seek the help of your partner, or a neighbour or friend, to ensure that the childrens' needs are met.

When the fateful morning arrives don't have the alarm clock set to wake you. Unplug the telephone, if there is no one else in the house, so that the telephone will not distract you. Do not take the phone off the hook, just unplug it. If anyone rings they will get a continuous ringing tone as though you were not at home, which to all intents and purposes you are not. If there is anyone else in the house, do not talk to them, and ask them beforehand not to engage you in conversation.

If you lie in bed you may find yourself feeling very uncomfortable and your feet will not stay still. Your mind may tell you that this is a ridiculous experiment and a waste of time. Do not jettison the experiment. Instead, get up and fix yourself a light breakfast. After breakfast, sit in a comfortable chair. If you begin to think again that this is ridiculous, just stay with the thought but do not allow it to stop the experiment. If you are a religious person and you are thinking of yourself as selfish and neglectful of duties, remind yourself that this experiment is, in fact, biblically based. You are having a sabbath. Even God rested on the seventh day.

By lunchtime you may notice how tired your eyes feel and you may wish to sleep. Go with this feeling, eat the lunch you prepared, and then have a sleep. By the evening you may well be in a more comfortable frame of mind, and be able to enjoy the silence and the chance to think about the experiment you are carrying out. Do not use the time to think through problems at work or elsewhere. If such problems enter your consciousness do not dwell on them. Simply acknowledge them and then direct your thoughts back to the experiment you are carrying out.

For the following morning, set your alarm an hour earlier than you are used to arising. Use this hour to write up the experiment. Whether you use the hour literally writing or just mentally writing it up, evaluate what you have learned. What were the feelings and thoughts you experienced? You may begin to get clues as to what your busy lifestyle is enabling you to avoid.

Did you feel depressed, tired, and lonely? Perhaps you are more tired than you realised. A busy life can make you insensitive to bodily sensations which draw your attention to tiredness. If you became depressed, perhaps you felt hopeless and desperate, or angry and guilty. It might be that you became angry with me for designing this experiment, and suggesting you go through with it when everything inside told you that it was wrong and selfish. Perhaps you also felt controlled and hemmed in by my instructions. These feelings are remnants from your childhood. Perhaps you are beginning to learn how much you still live there emotionally, and how difficult it is to take responsibility for your actions now, in the same way that you experienced your parents as reneging on their responsibilities. I am happy to accept responsibility for setting up the experiment but you are responsible for carrying it out.

Did you enjoy the day? If you did, what can you learn from this?

● Perhaps your busy lifestyle is an attempt to block out fun from your life.

● Perhaps all the activity you engage in functions to keep your nose to the grindstone, in case you otherwise discover that life can be enjoyable and that your company can be good company for you. As a child, life may have been very serious indeed, and any fun was tinged with fear that things might get out of control.

● Perhaps you are learning for the first time that your seriousness and earnestness is a mask you wear to reassure people around you that you are suffering as much as they are when, inside, the opposite is true.

● Perhaps as a child you felt guilty when you enjoyed yourself. You may have carried on with the guilt but submerged the joy.

- Perhaps the day was a combination of all sorts of feelings and thoughts. Write these down either mentally or physically with a pen and paper. Put question marks beside them. You will only be able to understand a fraction of these feelings and thoughts. That doesn't matter; what does matter is that you took a risk and began to experiment.

If you can grasp the principle of experimentation to learn about yourself and others, then you have grasped a very important tool to use in furthering your recovery.

It is important that you thank those who assisted in your experiment. If they are safe people you may gain enormously by sharing the outcome of the experiment with them. If they are not safe people they may well still be curious, in which case you can tell them as much as it feels safe to tell them. Your recovery will be enhanced enormously if you can keep those who are close to you informed of your progress. People may become resentful if they feel they are being excluded and may not wish to help you. If your spouse or partner has had to make sacrifices to facilitate your experiment, it might be helpful to offer to return the compliment.

13: *Taking an observer role in your life deprives you of the benefit of full participation*

As a child I desperately wanted to be a professional footballer, and I spent a good deal of time playing football and practising my skills. At eleven years of age I got a football outfit of my favourite team for my Christmas present and spent all of Christmas Day running about on the local field scoring goals, and in complete rapture because I could make believe that I really was a great footballer playing for my favourite team. I wanted to sleep in my football gear and wear it every day. I remember my mother asking me where she should sew the team's emblem on the football shirt, and much to the amusement of my father and the rest of the family, I told her she must sew it on the left-hand side, next to my heart.

As time moved on, I began to realise that my dream would not be fulfilled. I was not skilful enough to make it as a professional footballer. Indeed, I had less than average skill. Instead, I became a passionate football spectator and remain one to this day. I am still aware, however, of a great desire to get on the field of play and when I go to see my favourite team play I feel my foot twitch when the ball enters the goal area as I volley the ball into the net alongside our centre-forward.

Many ACAs live their entire life in this way. They become spectators on the sidelines of their own lives and never get on to the field of play. This, of course, enormously limits their emotional and social life. Michael, the man who could not play with his children, felt like a spectator in regards to his fathering role with his children. His recovery was quite literally about getting on to the field of play with them and becoming a participant.

Recovery is about getting on to the field of play, whatever that might mean in your life, rather than being an eternal spectator. This is why recovery can only truly take place in ordinary relationships. Psychotherapy and self-help groups are invaluable aids, but the relationships formed there, vital as they are, are not recovery in themselves.

14: It is important to distinguish between limitations and barriers

In my case I had to come to terms with a very real limitation – that I was not good enough as a footballer to play professionally. Many ACAs live their emotional and social lives as though they have severe limitations when, in fact, they have created barriers within themselves.

For example, when ACAs encounter anxiety and fear in an intimate relationship they can begin to withdraw, and to limit the intimacy they will allow. They then conclude that there is something wrong with them because they are so frightened and anxious. They believe that they can be close to no one, that their overwhelming feelings indicate an inherent incapacity.

Recovery is about reaching a point where you are not pushed about by internal feelings. Rather, that fear and anxiety are signals to you that something is dangerous or uncertain. It becomes a question of understanding what the danger is and what the uncertainty is about. Such fears and anxieties may be well founded.

- Perhaps the person you are involved with is untrustworthy and abusive. The anxiety and fear are your friends because they enable you to know who to trust and who not to trust, whether to continue in a relationship or not.

- Perhaps the anxiety and fear are unfounded in the present relationship; they belong to your past. They may be connected to an inner saboteur who is determined to avoid closeness and intimacy, in the interests of maintaining an inner stability founded on the adaptations made to your alcoholic family.

You will need to decide whether you want to risk disruption and instability in your inner world and the discomfort this will bring, as a price worth paying for growth and development, or whether you are not yet ready for such discomfort.

Remember, recovery is not compulsory; you can decide to remain in dysfunction. If you do decide that you want recovery and suffer temporary discomfort in the interests of growing, then speak to your partner and let him or her know that you must go slowly and carefully through this phase with them. S/he may want to help you, and share with you how s/he overcame such fears in his/her own life. If your partner cannot accept how difficult this phase is for you then you may need to find a new partner who can.

What is clear, is that the statement, 'I can't get close to people because I am limited in the intimacy I can have,' needs to be replaced by: 'I won't get close to people because my fears and anxieties present barriers which seem so great.' In this way, you can choose to overcome the barriers, no matter how long this takes or at what cost, or take responsibility for staying stuck in the prison of your childhood fears and anxieties.

Finding your own path

Do not worry if you have not understood some or all of these principles. Don't be afraid to experiment and find your own path. They are offered to you from my experience. There are others who have different experiences that you might find more helpful. The important thing is that you take charge of your own recovery and begin your own journey.

I spent the first two years of my recovery in depression, and I was eight years into recovery before I accepted a more overtly spiritual path. My recovery, like so many others, began as a rather desperate struggle; then it turned into a journey of discovery and eventually into an adventure. Today I can still find myself struggling with the feeling that I have learnt nothing. I am thankful for this now rather than disheartened, because it reminds me of my own fallibility and the need to continue to grow and learn. The more I have learned, the more I have become aware of how much more there is to learn. Life is indeed an adventure!

CHAPTER 7

The Stages of Recovery

Now I will outline the process of recovery, because recovery from codependency – that is, from the adaptations you made to the dysfunction in your alcoholic family – usually proceeds in an orderly, predictable way. We shall also consider some specific barriers to recovery and some special cases. Even if you are not an ACA you might find the principles helpful because they can be applied to all sorts of situations.

Whatever the nature and content of an individual journey in recovery there is an identifiable and consistent path that ACAs traverse in the course of recovery.[1] It consists of five stages.

1: Surviving

This does not look markedly different from the path taken by the alcoholic in the throes of his addiction. The alcoholic continues to drink to avoid feeling even more sick – he knows that if he stops drinking he will go into unpleasant withdrawals – so he continues in denial. The early stage of abstinence makes the alcoholic feel much worse than if he continued drinking. Thus denial seems to be the best way to achieve survival.

ACAs who continue to deny that their parent is an alcoholic are applying a similar logic. So long as there is no problem, nothing need be done about it. All the pent up pain and emotion can be kept intact so long as no admission is made. The ACA who can drop his/her denial about a parent's alcoholism may then move on to a second, sub-stage. While admitting that the parent may have been an alcoholic, the child insists that he or she was not affected – or only minimally so. This is denial none the less.

In such circumstances, you may keep bottled up all of the anger and sadness that the admission of parental alcoholism might bring forth; the powerfulness of denial can be so great. I have witnessed many an ACA who was ready to lash out at anyone who would defile a parent's name with the label of alcoholism, let alone acknowledge that they have been affected. It is a bit like the king who cuts off the head of the messenger who brings bad news. The anger is displaced from the news on to the person who brings it. Mostly, you will stay in the survivor stage until you reach 'rock bottom', when it becomes more uncomfortable to remain in denial of problems than it is to acknowledge them.

- It became too painful for Michael to remain in denial about the effect of his childhood experiences and how they affected his own relationship with his children. He engaged in therapy only because it was more painful not to do so.

- It took the death of two of Neil's friends before he was able to relinquish denial of his heroin addiction, and afterwards it was only his intense fear which motivated him to look at his codependency.

- Jenny had to face the catastrophe of her son's suicide attempt before she was ready to face her alcoholism, and her renewed drinking prompted her to recognise that stopping drinking by itself would only lay the foundation of her recovery and not secure it.

Rock bottom experiences There are two sorts of 'rock bottom' experience:

- A low rock bottom occurs when all has been lost because of an addiction or codependency. Physical or mental health may be lost and you become ready to face change.

● A high 'rock bottom' occurs when you realise that a great deal more might be lost if the problems are not addressed. For example, someone who has been smoking heroin injects for the first time. Suddenly there is a realisation that one is on a slippery slope and the addiction must be faced before it can progress any further.

If you are an ACA reading this book, and being reached for the first time, there is an opportunity to face a high 'rock bottom' as you drop your denial and begin the process of change before any further losses are incurred. If you can do this, you will enter the identification stage.

2: Identification

When Michael reached this stage, he did something which is characteristic at this point – his story came flooding out. Once he relinquished denial, there was literally a cascade of feelings and experiences which he became aware of and began to express. It was a bit as if someone had released a pressure valve.

Many ACAs have this experience. Some become very frightened, because they are unused to such strong feelings and they discover, too, that they have feelings that they never thought they had. Anger, sadness, guilt and shame become evident. Others, however, far from being frightened by the outpourings, are relieved to have found a place where the feelings can be expressed. This can be a tremendous time of letting go and unburdening. Having named the beast – alcoholism – so much begins to fall into place.

The identification phase involves a more realistic assessment of the past and a reworking of one's relationship to willpower. At last, the family secret is out and the oppressive rules are being broken. The no talking, no feeling, no trusting rules are all hit for six. Many ACAs are on cloud nine as the honeymoon period of recovery has begun. However, some will not progress beyond this point. A new addiction may begin, an addiction to the high of recovery, for before any further progress can be made an honest appraisal of one's own codependent distortions must begin.

When Michael understood that it was his father's alcoholism which had affected his capacity to be a father, only half the job was done. He then had to go on to acknowledge how this fact expressed itself in his own life in the present time. Only when he could realise that it was expressed in destructive ways – in his wish to punish his children because he was envious of them – was he able to progress. Similarly, he was depriving his wife of sex to punish her for being like his mother. Only when he could see how his codependency was being enacted in his present life could he begin to be free of codependency.

Many ACAs only do half the work in this phase and become stuck at the point of realising how their parents affected them. They do not want to face how they are affecting their own relationships by continuing with dysfunctional patterns learned long ago. We are all happy to be perceived as wronged angels but find it difficult to see ourselves as wronging others. Later in this chapter I will return to this important point, because it is a barrier to further recovery that many do not overcome.

Neil, too, found this part of the identification stage very difficult to handle. He could look at his heroin addiction, and how his early losses affected him but he was very reluctant to look at his own destructiveness in relationships. His commitment to our work together saw him through this phase but it was touch and go. Although the vast majority of ACAs will never enter psychotherapy, either because they do not need it or because they are frightened of it, those who see psychotherapy as a process of pampering or indulgence get a nasty shock when they are asked to face up to their own destructiveness, and may discontinue therapy.

Finally, the identification stage crucially addresses the central issue of control. You give up trying to control what is beyond your grasp and instead concentrate on being effective. In this way, distortions caused to self-esteem through the excessive need to control others is replaced with self-esteem based on the capacity to change yourself and to become effective in your world.

3: Core issues

This stage is characterised by a deepening awareness of the limits of willpower and control. It involves an active exploration of the ways in which a refusal to admit powerlessness and the fear of being out of control is affecting your life. The leap of faith made to enter recovery is tested to the full. If delusions and distortions about control are relinquished, what is left? Sometimes a gnawing emptiness can take over and one is left in despair.

An alcoholic in treatment at St Joseph's Centre entered such a state towards the end of his treatment. He had metaphorically fallen into what he described as a black hole – dark, empty and all consuming. He felt completely alone and lost. Another member of his group then revealed that he, himself, had fallen into such a hole many times in the past. In such a position he did what he felt he could not do, that was to reach up with his hands, and he discovered that he could be rescued if he so wished. He suggested to the group that the choice was open to anyone in a black hole – to stay there for as long as s/he could bear it and when s/he could bear it no longer to reach out and to know s/he could be rescued, or to languish there forever, for lack of the action of reaching out.

Crucially, this stage of development hangs upon a growing ability to be responsible for oneself, to ask for what you need, and to take responsibility if you choose to remain alone and isolated. If the identification stage has been only half finished, in the way I have described, then this vital stage cannot be passed.

4: Integration

The transformations of attitude made during the previous phase are now woven into a new fabric. New belief systems develop. The child within becomes an integral part of the self-concept. Feelings are recognised as facts inside, neither to be judged nor got rid of; they just are. Pleasure is experienced in the presence of the self. You realise that you do not have to do things or control things to be of value. Your value lies in your own unique being.

Now, codependent traits can be put to good use. For example, all the intellectual defenses used to avoid recognition of problems can be turned into legitimate intellectual pursuits. Drama queens join amateur dramatics societies where they can apply their range of emotional expressions to entertaining themselves and others. Those who are extremely sensitive and have entered helping professions become more skilful as they apply their trait to their work. The integration stage becomes a time when survival traits are no longer used to avoid painful realities but rather they are turned on their heads and become life enriching.

The recovering codependent becomes far more interested in personal integrity than doing things to get a high or to be made happy. Peace of mind flows from the way life is being lived, rather than from the accomplishments achieved. Below is a 'bill of rights'[2], developed by an ACA during this phase, which you might find useful to your recovery. I certainly did.

● Life should have choices beyond mere survival.

● You have a right to say 'no' to anything when you feel you are not ready, or it is unsafe to say 'yes'.

● Life should not be motivated by fear.

● You have a right to all your feelings.

● You are probably not guilty.

● You have a right to make mistakes.

● There is no need to smile when you cry.

- You have a right to terminate conversations with people who make you feel put down and humiliated.

- You can be healthier than those around you.

- It's OK to be relaxed, playful, and frivolous.

- You have the right to change and grow.

- It is important to set limits and to be selfish.

- You can be angry at someone you love.

- You can take care of yourself, no matter what circumstances you are in.

5: *Genesis*

The final phase of recovery is called the genesis because it is about how the recovering ACA begins participating in the creation of his or her own world. The life that is produced is an accurate expression of the life that moves within. As such it will be different for each person and it is impossible to categorise the ways in which the ACA will develop. There are as many ways as there are people on the planet. It is our freedom and our liberation; the tyranny of codependency is over.

In the next chapter we will look at the aids that are available to assist the personal quest that recovery becomes. Before we do so, however, I want to cover a few more important points about recovery and barriers to it which are commonly encountered.

Survivor guilt

An important barrier to recovery encountered by many ACAs is that of survivor guilt – the term first used to describe the experience of Jews who survived the holocaust during the Second World War. Many survivors lost part or the whole of their families, who were murdered in the death camps. In response, they experienced severe depression and some even committed suicide. The difficulty stemmed from guilt at having been the one to survive.

As you begin to grow in recovery you can experience a very similar phenomenon, if other family members are still suffering from the effects of living in an alcoholic family system. Perhaps the alcoholic is still drinking or perhaps other family members have been so damaged that they do not have the will to recover. You feel guilty that you cannot share your recovery with other family members, to the extent that it may stunt your own growth. Although your concern is genuine, it can also mask a deeply embedded sense of unworthiness and shame.

If you find yourself in this position I suggest that you experiment with getting your whole family well. Try everything you possibly can, hold nothing back in your efforts to make them recover. Hide the alcoholic's drink, and rage at your whole family to see if you can force them into recovery, but put a time limit on your efforts. It might be a day, a week, or a month, but put a time limit on it, and then stand back to see what you have achieved. My guess is that you will have got nowhere, except to make yourself miserable. You might need to try this experiment over and over again before, finally, you become convinced that your efforts are futile. Please do it as many times as you need to, because if you have any lingering doubts you will be tempted to do it again anyway.

In this process, you will learn from your own experience about your powerlessness and the learning will be valuable. You will also be faced with your own uncertainty about your worthiness for recovery and this, too, will be of value. What purpose does your misery serve? Do you need to be punished some more? If you can honestly answer 'no' to this question then you will have resolved your survivor guilt and can begin to pick up from where you left off on your own journey of recovery. If you answer 'yes' to the need for more punishment, then perhaps you have been more damaged than you thought. Can you say how much more punishment you need? Can you put a limit on it? If you cannot answer this question, don't worry, just hold on to the question every time you are made miserable by your attempt to control your family. You may need professional help or perhaps you will reach a point where the question itself will lead you to let go of your family. Their time for recovery has not yet come, it may never come. This is the tragedy of family alcoholism.

The greatest gift you can give to your family is your continued recovery. In time, they may say to themselves 'What's happened to Mary/Martin, s/he seems different these days, more relaxed and happy than ever before?' At this point, you may be able to help. The more you work on your own recovery, the better the position you will be in to help other family members if, and when, their time comes to face up to themselves.

Grieving for losses

As recovery progresses, you begin to grieve for obvious losses. You can become surprised however if, having grieved for a lost father, for example, the sense of grief keeps returning. It is as though you are wanting to get it over with and put it behind you and your best efforts are being thwarted. Unfortunately, the more you grieve the more you become aware of the magnitude of the loss. It is not uncommon for ACAs well into recovery to become aware of even greater reservoirs of unexpressed grief than they had ever imagined could be contained within them. You can become aware of deep, deep sadness about losses. You never realised before quite how much you had lost.

It is vital to remember that the grieving is being done on behalf of the child within. As recovery progresses the child becomes more and more able to tell his/her story, and it is the story of a child suffering great loss. Your child did not have your adult knowledge when these losses were sustained. Your child within was overwhelmed by them and needs time now to tell you how bad it all was. If you say that you want it all over in a day, this sends a signal to the child that he or she is to be oppressed yet again. The child will retreat for a while and then emerge once again. That is why the grief recurs over and over again. The less you try to tell the child that he or she has grieved enough, the more quickly he or she can get on with the story and the more quickly you can integrate the experience into your larger self. My work with Neil, the songwriter, provides an extreme example of how grieving is about the losses experienced as a child.

Neil lost his father when he was a very young child. He suffered a double blow when his mother turned to alcohol, and was lost to him too. When Neil started to talk about this time, tears began to trickle down his cheek. As the session ended, he told me that he was glad that he had grieved at last for his father. He thought that it was all over.

The next session was two days later. He arrived late, with a blanket around him, and told me he did not know what was happening to him. He felt paralysed with fear and had an enormous lump in his throat. The lump was very painful but he did not feel that he could clear his throat because the lump was so large that it might cut him to ribbons.

Neil was beginning to experience his loss not as a grown adult but as a young child. Over the next three weeks we met daily and had telephone contact each evening. A friend of his moved in with him so that he would not have to be alone.

Over this time we worked hard to provide safety for the child within him who was feeling so frightened. Although he did express some sadness and anger, the point of our work was not to achieve a great outpouring of feeling about the loss of his father, but rather to provide a safe structure around such feelings.

In his childhood, Neil had effectively had a nervous breakdown, not because his grief was so great, but because he could not experience his grief safely. His mother's withdrawal meant that he was unsupported in his grieving. The work of the therapy was not to facilitate the grieving per se, but to provide support so that his own natural grieving attempts could function in safety, at a later time.

Over the following four months, Neil began to feel more of the deep sadness at his loss and the intense anger he had built up against his alcoholic mother. He had a further episode of intense fear and paralysis as he became more and more aware of the enormity of what had happened to him as a very young child. When he emerged, he was once more able to experience the sadness and anger. However, I would judge the success of the therapy not on how much grieving was facilitated but rather on his capacity to grieve in safety.

Neil's example, although extreme, illustrates the nature of grieving. It is not a once and for all event. The more grieving we do, the more capable of grieving we become. In time, the memory of a lost parent becomes a kind of sweet sadness. We experience our love for them and are enriched by the thought of them. We are no longer frightened by what is, after all, a very natural process.

The sexually abused

Some ACAs will have experienced sexual abuse in childhood. Sometimes the abuse has been perpetuated by the drinking parent, who, in a state of intoxication has lost a grip on any moral or ethical standard and perceives the child as an extension of himself. Therefore, the parent feels justified in using the child for sexual gratification. Sometimes, too, the alcoholic becomes so isolated from adult contact that he prefers to relate to children. Children are trusting and loving, no matter how the adult behaves.

Sometimes, the abuser is not the alcoholic parent, but because the parents are so wrapped up in the alcoholism they fail in their duty to protect their children from those who might be abusive. Jenny and her sister were not adequately protected from their parents' party guests, who would intrude into the girls' bedroom during Saturday night parties. Jenny had her bottom patted by one such intruder, and although many people would not define this behaviour as sexual abuse, it had quite an impact on Jenny and her sister.

Jenny's difficulty with achieving orgasm was connected to the lack of safety she experienced during sexual contact.

Many would say that the party guest meant no harm and was merely being friendly. However, we cannot define abuse according to the attitude of the abuser. Most abusers carry out their acts with the best intentions. Hitler thought he was doing the world a favour by killing Jews, for example.

Similarly, we cannot define sexual abuse by describing some acts as abusive and others as not, because such definitions do not take into account more insidious forms of abuse. For example, the father who leers at his teenage daughter, or makes constant remarks about the shape of her breasts is being highly abusive. Although no sexual contact is taking place the teenager is being invaded and intruded upon, and is truly being abused.

My limited clinical experience of treating people who have been sexually abused is that the abuse is rarely subtle. You do not have to go out of your way to uncover it. It is my experience, too, that those who witness sexual abuse can be as affected as those who have been actually abused.

Many of the adaptations that take place in childhood to cope with parental alcoholism are remarkably similar to those that take place when children are sexually abused but there is no obvious drug or alcohol problem. Children who are sexually abused keep a family secret in the same way that children who live in alcoholic families protect a secret. The adaptations that take place in the inner worlds of sexually abused children are also similar. Parts of the child's self are submerged and hidden away for protection and the parent is preserved as 'good'.

However, there are also important extra problems experienced by ACAs who have been sexually abused:

- They can experience greater degrees of disturbance in adulthood.

- They are more likely to be self-destructive to a greater degree than other ACAs. For example, they may cut themselves and abuse their bodies more. (ACAs do not typically become self-abusive in this way.)

- They also have a greater propensity to develop eating disorders.

- They display far greater distortions in their sexual identity and sexual behaviour.

So what can be said to those who have been sexually abused? If you the reader have been sexually abused, what can be understood about your predicament?

- Firstly, you probably feel a great sense of guilt. This guilt is important and will not be removed by injunctions that say you were not responsible. Your guilt is your way of believing that you could have prevented or altered what happened. If you did not have this guilt then you would probably feel in a worse position because you would have to feel all the pain of your powerlessness. Your guilt is a way of trying to master something; it is a protective device and you are right to hold on to it until it is safe to let it go. It will become safe only when you can be sure you are capable of taking responsibility for the pain of your powerlessness. Only when you feel secure with safe people and safe places is it realistic to let go of the guilt.

- Secondly, there is the problem of shame. You might well have asked yourself the question, why me? Why have I been sexually abused but not someone else? You may have come to the conclusion that there is something about you and your sexuality which provoked the abuse. This, too, is a protective device which you must not relinquish until you are ready, because the alternative is to blame the parent for the abuse, and unleash the full expression of your rage. In so doing, you would greatly disturb the balance of your mind which has preserved the parent as good so as to ensure your survival.

- Thirdly, there is the problem of rage. When you feel safe, the rage will emerge as you become aware of the absolute hideousness of the violation that has occurred. It is important that you express your rage. Later you will be able to separate the person from his behaviour, and heal the hurt.

The sexually abusive

If you are sexually abusing a child or young person, then you may well be putting into action what happened to you as a child or what you saw happening then. Don't continue because you think the damage is already done or because you believe that you are evil and can't be helped. You, too, are trying to master something which happened to you many years ago, and you, too, can take responsibility for yourself and your actions. Children who are sexually abused suffer just as much from the denial of abuse as the abuse itself. It will make a difference to yourself as well as to the child, if you can verify that the abuse took place. For then you can both be helped.

The physically abused

Alcoholic families can be violent places. In Chapter 1 you read the accounts of the Scottish teenagers who had been physically abused. The smacking and hitting out can be signs of the tension boiling over, or simply the excesses of behaviour resulting from states of intoxication. Consistent physical abuse lowers your sensitivity to violence and you may come to see it as part and parcel of ordinary behaviour.

In recent years there has been an important shift in the attitude towards the physical abuse of children. It is no longer OK for schools to administer physical punishments, although we still tolerate it in the home. In time I would hope that this, too, will become not OK.

In your alcoholic family you may have witnessed or been subjected to a particular sort of violence, when someone loses their temper and appears to get out of control. You began to fear for your safety and indeed your life. This can interfere with recovery because you never learned that anger can be expressed openly but without fear that it will explode into violence or get out of hand.

It is important to understand that there are limits to our anger. We can safely express it even if it contains violence of extreme sorts. One person I know simply wrote it down, so that it became external to her and therefore manageable. You may have to experiment to find ways of externalising your anger. Perhaps you can write things down or perhaps you will find some other way. Some people use vigorous physical exercise to let off steam. Playing squash, or hitting a punch-bag are other effective ways of dissipating anger, safely.

The physically abusive

If you have become physically abusive yourself then it will impede your recovery if you continue in this way. If you are abusive to a spouse you are very much stuck in trying to exert power over people. You cannot make people love you or respect you. If you hit them they may react as you want them to through fear but secretly they will hate you and will look for revenge. Children who witness such abuse learn that violence is a way of getting their own way, and that getting your own way is the most important thing in life.

Children who are beaten by their parents when they are naughty are far more likely to learn to avoid detection rather than what the difference is between right and wrong. They will learn to lie and to have 'accidents' more and more as they seek to avoid a good hiding.

There is another important reason to stop beating children, and it involves carrying out a further experiment. If you do not believe that children do not learn the difference between right and wrong through physical punishment, then each time you hit your children for doing wrong, write down the mood you were in before you were provoked to anger. If I am correct, you will find that you hit your children when you are most under stress – when you and your partner have just had a row, or when you have had a bad day at work, or some other factor external to the child's behaviour. The child learns that punishment is an arbitrary thing, and will try to keep you in a good mood so as to avoid the risk of beatings.

Recovery is about being responsible for yourself and your actions. Your children will learn more about right and wrong by the way you live your life than by any physical punishment.

The emotionally abused

Emotional abuse and neglect are quite common in alcoholic families. We can define emotional abuse as interactions which are offensive. Being offensive means intruding upon another without concern for his or her feelings or thoughts. Here is a story to illustrate this act of offence.

As a treat, a family goes out to a restaurant for a meal. The waitress comes to take their order. The little girl asks for hamburger and chips. The mother tells the waitress that the little girl really wants stew with vegetables. The little girl then orders an ice cream sundae for dessert. Her mother tells the waitress that she really wants fresh fruit salad. The waitress asks the child what she would like to drink, and she replies 'coke'; her mother instructs the waitress to bring milk. After ten minutes the waitress returns with the food, bringing the little girl a hamburger, chips and coke. In delight and surprise, she turns to her mother and says, 'Look Mummy, that waitress thinks I really exist!'

Although this story is not true, it illustrates the nature of emotional abuse. Children who are denied a separate existence from their parents never develop an understanding of their own needs and wants. Many in recovery find difficulty in knowing the difference, and others still draw a blank when they ask themselves what they want or need. Recovering a sensitivity to your needs and wants takes time. It is important to experiment and to continue to identify the strands which underly the ups and downs of your life. Making new mistakes is important, too, as they give you new information and new learning about yourself.

Emotional abuse and neglect in alcoholic families is frequently more obvious and blatant. Remember the single parent who confined her child to a playpen for days at a time while she herself went on a bender? This is the more obvious sort of offensive behaviour that you may have been aware of in your past life.

Another form of emotional abuse which may be difficult to appreciate, is that it can be perpetrated not by what is done but by what is not done. As a psychotherapist hearing many ACAs tell their stories, I listen to what is said but also to what is not said. As in the famous Sherlock Holmes story, *The Hound of the Baskervilles*, where he discovers the answer to the mystery by observing that the 'dog did not bark in the night', so it can be when listening to ACAs tell their story. It is not so much what happened but what did not happen which is crucial:

- The young child who is never physically held or played with.

- The teenager who is never given recognition when she achieves things.

- The young adult who is cut off and not spoken to when s/he begins to assert him or herself.

The transactions are real, and cause great offence but cannot really be understood.

The emotionally abusive

If you emotionally abuse your children they are unlikely to tell you how much that hurts. But they will probably display problem behaviour at school or at home, or they will be excessively compliant and 'good'. Such children are using survival tactics to preserve themselves as best they can. This situation can and will change over time, so long as you embark upon, and continue in, recovery. You can not 'undo' the situation which led to the present problem. You can only acknowledge to yourself and to them that problems have existed in the family which were not of their making but for which they have paid a price. As much as you might feel guilt about this, telling the children, in language they can understand and in ways that are age appropriate, will help to make real for them what they felt was unreal.

If you are an alcoholic ACA in recovery, then you will need to explain that your drinking and the behaviour which followed was a result of the disease of alcoholism. If you reach out in this way your children will be touched – but their behaviour may not change for a long time. They will need to check out your recovery and reassure themselves that it is not yet another false promise.

It will not help your children if you give lavish gifts to make up to them for what has happened. What they really need is for you to achieve continued recovery and become consistent in your behaviour towards them. You must be prepared to be their parent and to encourage them to be your children. The greatest gift you can give them is your time and attention.

If you are not an alcoholic but an ACA who decided that you would do better than your parents at child rearing, you have probably discovered that you have become more like them than is comfortable for you. Remember, recovery is about living in the present; you can not change what has happened in the past. But as you make time to listen to your own needs and wants you will become more able to listen to your children, and hear what it is they need and want of you.

The NSPCC have an annual 'Listen to Children Week'. Perhaps this year you can take part in this experiment and give your children more time and attention than you are used to giving them. My seven-year-old daughter drew my attention to this annual event. She helped me to understand that I do not listen enough to my own children. I, too, still struggle with this.

Getting stuck

The point at which many ACAs get stuck in their recovery is at the identification stage, as outlined earlier in this chapter. Having become aware of the impact of family alcoholism, you are able to unburden yourself of many years of pent up feelings. You will experience the liberation of finally understanding why you have been miserable, empty, or lost, or whatever the presenting problem might have been. You have gained insight into your problems and are able to understand many of the reasons why you feel as you do. Many changes take place as you commit yourself to the path of recovery. Then you progress no further.

Some are content with the gains made and have no wish to go further. Your emotional life may have been opened up sufficiently to allow you to live a far more comfortable life than you ever thought possible and you have no great motivation to go further. If this is the case, then this is fine and the best of luck to you.

Others do not progress beyond this point for quite different reasons. One is that they are frightened to look too closely at how codependent patterns are acted out in present relationships because it means acknowledging not only what has happened but also how closely they enact the same patterns in their own lives. For example, there are ACAs who punish their parents mercilessly for having subjected them to merciless punishment as children. ACAs in this position seek to justify their actions rather than question them. They feel exonerated because they believe that their parents deserve to be punished for having been such bad parents. These ACAs forget that alcoholism is a disease and that recovery is about living in today. They do not want to face their real motive, which is revenge and self-justification. Those ACAs who persist in punishing their parents continue the act of abuse not only towards the parents but also towards themselves. They have become brutalised by their experiences.

A further reason that some ACAs get stuck is because they do not feel that they deserve full recovery. Their shame is so deeply ingrained that they settle for less. Classically, they mistake barriers for limitations and begin to self-destruct just as they are about to move forwards. They display the feature of never completing a project, as outlined in Chapter 4 when we looked at the characteristics of adult children. They feel frightened to move above what they perceive to be their level in life, and success poses more problems than failure, or so it would appear.

If you are in this position you very much need the encouragement of safe people. You may also need practical help in completing projects, even though all your instincts tell you not to ask for help and you become isolated and frozen with fear. Applying the principle of experimentation outlined in Chapter 6 may be very helpful to you in moving on.

The spiritual path

A major obstacle to recovery for many is the notion that they must adopt spiritual values in order to grow away from the effects of alcoholic parenting. You may baulk at this prospect. I certainly did when I first encountered it, so it is important to understand precisely what we mean by the spiritual path. First of all, it is important to know why alcoholism itself is a disease of the spirit.

Alcoholism as a spiritual disease   As the disease of alcoholism progresses, the behaviour of the alcoholic shows a marked decline in moral and ethical standards. He may lie, cheat and steal in the service of his addiction. While drinking, he may become involved in sexual and social practices which appal him when he is sober. He may ask himself: 'How can I have descended to this level?' as he begins to see the price he pays for continued addiction. In part, it is this decline in standards of behaviour which leads us to call alcoholism a 'spiritual disease'. Progressively, it erodes the person's moral and ethical fibre. However, there is a second and perhaps more important reason.

At their deepest level, alcoholics have fallen into a very ambivalent relationship with themselves, and with life and death. They seem unable to make a commitment to life and yet, at the same time, they are frightened of death and uncommitted to the path of self-destruction along which their drinking leads them.

In the final stages of addiction they hate drinking and yet are so full of self-loathing that they hate life itself and will not stop. They enter into a world of despair and, ultimately, psychosis and death. As their bodies and minds are destroyed, so also their spirit seems to be destroyed. By spirit, I mean a willingness and commitment to live. The spirit may be destroyed long before the body and mind are destroyed. We say of such people: 'the lights are on but there's nobody home.'

If we retrace our steps, this death of spirit is not surprising. Alcoholics can be very grandiose, full of false pride, and perfectionistic. They also have a very distorted perception of willpower. When things start going wrong they are unable to comprehend that it has anything to do with them and their drinking. How could it be? They are perfect and it is others who are messing up their lives.

Eventually, the alcoholic becomes defeated in his attempts to control his drinking. He sees this as an affront to his willpower and his world view which, of course, places him at the centre of events. He faces a crisis which can lead to recovery or to the continued progression of the disease. If the alcoholic can come to believe that he is suffering from an illness which defies the effort of the will because he is powerless over it, then he can begin to see himself in a more realistic perspective and the spirit will be revived; that is, he will find the willingness and commitment to live. Spiritual recovery, then, means a fundamental readjustment of the whole range of relationships that define who we are, and the assumptions made about our relationship to ourselves.

In this adjusted state the alcoholic may experience a profound spiritual awakening that seems to go beyond internal psychological adjustments. He begins to feel connected to a living God who is reaching out to him and wishes to make contact. There is a very vivid account of such an experience in the 'big book' of Alcoholics Anonymous.[4] As you read it, notice the crisis point when the subject asks himself, 'who are you to say there is no God', because it is at this point of readjustment in his internal relationship to himself that he finds humility which, in turn, facilitates the remarkable experience which follows. Such powerful and immediate experiences are rare.

'Our friend was a minister's son. He attended church school, where he became rebellious at what he thought was an overdose of religious education. For years thereafter he was dogged by trouble and frustration. Business failure, insanity, fatal illness, suicide in his immediate family embittered and depressed him. Post-war disillusionment, ever more serious alcoholism, impending mental and physical collapse, brought him to the point of self-destruction.

'One night, when confined in a hospital, he was approached by an alcoholic who had known a spiritual experience. Our friend was angered and cried out: "If there is a God, he certainly hasn't done anything for me!" But later, alone in his room he asked himself: "Is it possible that all the religious people I have known are wrong?" While pondering the answer he felt as though he lived in hell. Then, like a thunderbolt, a great thought came. It crowded out all else: "Who are you to say there is no God?"

'He tumbled out of his bed and on to his knees, overwhelmed by a conviction of the presence of God. It poured over and through him with the certainty and majesty of a great tide at flood. The barriers he had built through the years were swept away and he stood in the presence of Infinite Power and Love. For the first time, he lived in conscious companionship with his Creator.

'Thus was his cornerstone fixed in place. No later vicissitude has shaken it. His alcoholic problem was taken away. Save for a few brief moments the thought of drink has never returned; and at such times a great revulsion has risen up in him. Seemingly he could not drink even if he would. God had restored his sanity. What is this but a miracle of healing? Yet its elements are simple. Circumstances made him willing to believe. He humbly offered himself to his Maker – then he knew.'

Most alcoholics do not have such a profound experience. It is more likely that, over time, if they adopt the broadly spiritual approach practised by Alcoholics Anonymous, then their values will gradually change and become more spiritual.

They will learn to love life for its own sake, and this will be sufficiently spiritual for them.

ACAs and spiritual awakening

ACAs entering recovery follow a similar path to the alcoholic entering recovery. They, too, must relinquish denial and get their life into a new perspective. Being powerful over others in order to control them becomes part of the old way of doing things. ACAs must come to a new understanding of will power and its limitations, and thus the same opportunity for spiritual growth can be present as in the case of the alcoholic entering recovery. In time, ACAs, too, may find themselves aware of a higher presence reaching out to them and beckoning them into a closer union. It is entirely a matter of personal choice as to whether or not one answers such a calling.

Many dangers are associated with spiritual awakenings or rather what might appear to be spiritual awakenings. ACAs are particularly vulnerable to philosophies which offer instant enlightenment. These feed on the ACA's impulsiveness and eliminate the need to develop patience and discipline. ACAs are also vulnerable to philosophies which emphasise the 'oneness of all creation', because it feeds their most regressive impulses. Instead of defining themselves more clearly and achieving separation and individuation, ACAs opt for a merger with all things and return to an infantile state.

ACAs are vulnerable to philosophies which suggest that God is within you, and therefore you are at one with God. Many ACAs have lived their lives trying to attain the status of mini Gods or controllers of the universe, so such a philosophy only emphasises their codependent inclinations. In my view, the New Age philosophies embody many of these ideas and should be avoided by the recovering ACA. ACAs that I know who have gone down this path seem to have entered a cul-de-sac.

I believe that the philosophy which will offer most to ACAs is one that emphasises 'you' not as a deity but as a vulnerable and fallible human being. It should also challenge you to grow.

Ultimately, the choice is yours. Many ACAs find a perfectly good recovery from codependency and do not develop in any overtly spiritual way. Spirituality can become a drug or an escape unless you are careful about the path you are following and the company you keep on your journey. Whichever path you decide to take, I hope it proves as challenging and enriching as mine has been. I want to end this chapter with a story written by an unknown author. It is entitled *Footprints*.

Footprints

One night a man had a dream. He dreamed he was walking along the beach with the Lord. Across the sky flashed scenes from his life. For each scene, he noticed two sets of footprints in the sand: one belonging to him, and the other to the Lord.

When the last scene of his life flashed before him, he looked back at the footprints in the sand. He noticed that many times along the path of his life there was only one set of footprints. He also noticed that it happened at the very lowest and saddest times in his life.

This really bothered him and he questioned the Lord about it. 'Lord, you said that once I decided to follow you, you would walk with me all of the way. But I have noticed that at the most troublesome times in my life, there is only one set of footprints. I don't understand why, when I needed you most, you would leave me.'

The Lord replied. 'My son. My precious child. I love you and I would never leave you. During your times of trial and suffering, when you see only one set of footprints, it was then that I carried you.'

CHAPTER 8

Aids to Recovery

THERE are now a growing number of ways in which those seeking to come to terms with – and develop away from – the effects of parental drinking *can* be helped. There is a wide range of helpful literature, self-help groups throughout the UK and a variety of professional services, some of which specialise in working with adult children of alcoholics and other codependents.

Chapter 6 examined the ideas of safe places and safe people, and the role of the mentor. We now need to expand the safe people idea by characterising other important roles which might facilitate the process of healing, and pinpoint their strengths, weaknesses and applicability. As you consider whether *you* need help, this may assist you to structure your thinking.

The idea that safe people might fulfil roles arises from studying children who have suffered abuse of various sorts, and with adults struggling to come to terms with the effects of childhood abuse, including many from families where drugs and alcohol were an integral part of the dysfunctional pattern.

When facing up to troublesome events in childhood, such as the effects of parental alcoholism, all adult children can be aided by people and resources performing one or more key roles at different points along the path of recovery.[1] These roles are: the comforter, the interpreter/translator, the witness, and the advocate, thus emphasising the esssential qualities of each. No person or resource can be 100% in their particular role or roles all of the time. The best that can be hoped is that they can be 'good enough' and function 'well enough' for 'enough of the time'.

The comforter

This person can be vital at key points in recovery. S/he is likely to be a close friend who can be relied upon to give you time and attention for short periods at short notice – someone you could even ring at three in the morning, if you became distressed or frightened. As denial and minimisation recede and the full impact of feelings is allowed into awareness, you may well experience short periods of intense and overwhelming anxieties and fears. As contact is made with your cut-off and repressed 'child within', grief for the losses of your childhood comes to the surface and you may be overwhelmed with sadness, rage, guilt, or shame.

These feelings are intense because they are the feelings of the child within, struggling to be healed and become an integral part of you. If you are used to numbing out such feelings or denying their existence, then their appearance in such intensity can be very frightening. Some people think they are going mad, or that if they allow such feelings full expression they will not be able to regain their 'sanity' or former perspective. However, all such feelings are valid; if they feel real then they *are* real to you. If we stand in judgement upon them and deny them expression because we think they are childish or selfish, we impede or totally block recovery. Our feelings simply *are*, full stop.

Experiencing strong feelings introduces a new perspective or experience and this may seem strange and alien at first, demanding a lot of attention. But, over time, it will be integrated into the greater whole of 'the self'. It is a bit like seeing the Berlin Wall being demolished. At the time, it took all our attention. It was exciting and novel, to have the unimaginable happen in front of our eyes. Now it seems merely a distant flicker, because we have integrated it into our wider experience.

Fears and anxieties about strong feelings entering consciousness can be misplaced, in the sense that what is happening is that these feelings were always there anyway but have been intensified and distorted because they were pushed down for so long. These intense experiences also refer to events which took place in the past and the events themselves are over. It is a bit like someone who has had a grenade tossed into their living room and has been injured by the blast. They need to have their wounds dressed and their broken bones set, and to recover from the trauma.

When we reject our strong feelings it is akin to reacting to the blast by boarding up the room so that it can't happen again. Another reaction might be to become preoccupied with the injustice of it all and refuse to accept that what has happened has happened and cannot be undone. In this state of delusion the injured person metaphorically refuses to dress wounds, because the wounds can not be allowed to exist. However, the wounds do exist, they are painful, and they will not get better unless they are given due attention. Indeed they could fester and become even more serious. The situation can only be made better when a decision is made to survey the extent of the damage, to feel the pain that is there, and to recognise the need for help.

The comforter is someone who will support your expression of feelings and make it safe for you when you are frightened. A comforter needs no special training and most of us know of at least one person who could be contacted at short notice to spend time with us. It may be a spouse, a sibling or a close friend. A comforter needs to be mature, life-experienced, and able to understand the role you are asking them to fulfil. Ask them if they are prepared to take it on – do not wait until you are in a state and then simply 'dump' yourself on them.

Sex and comforters If you choose a comforter who is of the opposite sex, then you need to be aware that the intense feelings can have a powerful erotic component, because the desire to be comforted can include wanting to be held, touched, stroked, and loved in physical ways. Sexual contact and the close bodily union can be comforting and reassuring in a very special way. Literally sleeping with someone, and the warm touch of another's body next to us, is perhaps one of the most basic and satisfying forms of comfort.

However, entering into erotic contact with a comforter can be a means of escape from feelings which do not have an erotic basis. The desire for comfort and love can be very child-like and you could become frightened of – or embarrassed by – this and transform the child-like feelings into something 'more adult', such as erotic feelings. It may also be that this distinction between child-like neediness and adult eroticism has been blurred and confused by past experiences, either in childhood or more recently. For whatever reason, engaging in sexual contact with a comforter will not enable healing or recovery if such contact is an escape from child-like neediness. Furthermore, it becomes impossible for the comforter to stick to their task of providing comfort, if they are preoccupied with their own sexual gratification. It may also be that they are exploiting your vulnerability for their own ends, and their assumed role as comforter is bogus.

It is probably safer to choose a comforter who is not also a sexual partner, so that any holding or touching is not of a sexual nature. In this way, the two roles are less likely to become confused. Under no circumstances should you be persuaded that sexual contact has any part in a therapeutic relationship with a professional. In any case, it is unlikely that a professional would be in a position to take on the role of comforter. His/her role is to stay alongside while you experience the discomfort of feeling so needy and unworthy, and in this sense the professional's role is antithetical to the comforter.

The translator/interpreter

This should be someone who can make sense of your experiences when you can not, and help you to understand them. As we have already learned, many of the traits of codependency are attributable to growing up in certain sorts of family backgrounds. The interpreter must be someone with more experience than you have, someone who has 'been there' before, so that he or she can exercise judgement and provide informed opinion when you are faced with novelty and confusion.

The witness

This role calls for someone who is prepared to listen to your story, and to witness what has happeded to you, without interpreting or judging your experience. He or she simply acknowledges that you have been harmed or bruised as you describe it. He or she does not get angry on your behalf nor try to fix your pain. He or she simply listens and acknowledges that what has happened to you has happened and that you feel the way you do.

A witness is important, because telling your story is important. A witness validates the experience by being prepared to listen and to be with you as you talk. The witness may be the first person to whom you disclose your family secrets, and initially you may see yourself as 'betraying' these secrets; you will actually be freeing yourself of the great burden of your silence. New energy will be released which can be devoted to your recovery rather than to covering up for your dysfunctioning family.

The advocate

Here is someone who believes that you have a right to a life beyond mere survival, and that you have a right to your feelings, whatever these might be. He or she will support your right to have your own thoughts and to make your own decisions, no matter how foolish they might appear to others – or to you. S/he is capable of protesting on your behalf and insisting that your human rights are not compromised or infringed. An advocate can be strong on your behalf when you do not feel that you have the strength, or even the right, to have feelings or thoughts of your own.

Advocacy on behalf of the child within   Some forms of counselling and psychotherapy now proceed from the foundation of establishing advocacy for the child within. The principle applied is that the child within has been forced into hiding by the dysfunction in the family and needs to be coaxed out of hiding in order to make the adult whole and integrated in all his or her experience.

Having outlined the roles that suitable people might play in your recovery, let us now look at the various aids to recovery in this context.

Helpful literature

There is an enormous range of recovery books, mostly emanating from the USA. Unfortunately, they are of very variable quality and reflect a variety of theoretical orientations, from psychoanalytic to humanistic to religious. This can be a bit confusing, but if you persevere you will find an author or a particular orientation that you like and find helpful. You will find also that not only are there a variety of theoretical approaches but also a variety of practical steps advocated to achieve recovery and healing. It would be unrealistic to try to categorise the recovery literature here, rather I shall concentrate on the roles that books can play in recovery.

Comforters   To some extent, books can be comforting and uplifting, but they are not a source of intimate contact with another human being. Books tend to communicate predominantly with our intellect and our emotions, and although they can have a powerful impact, this is of a very different order from that which may be experienced in a functioning human relationship. The greatest comfort you are likely to find from reading books is the realisation that you are not alone, that others have been just as isolated and cut off. Recovery books almost always carry a message of hope and encouragement which can also be a comfort when you are feeling lost and desperate.

If you are at the beginning of your recovery, books might be the only acceptable way that you can find to explore your situation and find comfort. You may be very frightened of going to self-help groups and identifying with other adult children of alcoholics – the most difficult step many people face is going to their first meeting. You may experience massive internal resistance. You may be worried that someone will spot you going into a meeting and fear ridicule, or feel great shame at the prospect of identifying yourself as a codependent. You may feel that you have to be brave and strong, and not admit to a need for help. If you are in this frame of mind, books may be the best contact you can manage with your peers. After reading about others like yourself, your fear and shame might be reduced enough to enable you to make contact with another human being.

Books can also have an important role to play in interpreting our experiences. Recovery books provide a great deal of information on the nature of alcoholism and the various ways that ACAs can deal with these experiences. Books can be provocative in a positive way; I have probably learned more from those that I have taken exception to than those that I have enjoyed reading. It is good to be challenged in our thinking and beliefs. They are either confirmed and enriched by having to think them through anew or we are forced to change because we realise that we have no honest way of sustaining them.

Witnesses Books have a very limited role to play as witnesses because they cannot *listen* to your story. Even so, they may help you to see the value of witnessing as a role because, in effect, you are acting as a witness for the author and the people s/he is writing about.

Advocates Books can be a first important step towards discovering advocacy. The more you read, the more you may discover that you have rights beyond survival. Reading books may be the first step towards reaching out to others and allowing one of them to act as advocate for you.

An escape As recovery begins to take off and you move from recovery as a struggle to recovery as an adventure, books can play an important role. But beware! Intellectual pursuits can become an escape from practical daily recovery – reading more and more books can become a compulsion and sidetrack a balanced recovery.

Self-help groups

There are a variety of self-help groups available to ACAs entering recovery. All of those mentioned in this book are based on the belief that recovery from codependency can proceed from fellow sufferers meeting together to share their struggles, hope, strength and experience. The only requirement for membership is to have a desire to recover from the effects of another's drinking and dysfunctional behaviour.

Each group follows the 12-step programme for recovery discovered to be so effective in Alcoholics Anonymous groups for alcoholics with a desire to stop drinking. It is called a spiritual programme because it insists on a recognition of personal powerlessness over others and the need to seek help from a 'higher power', however this might be defined by the individual group member. It is neither religious nor sanctimonious but rather recognises and corrects the dysfunctional beliefs in alcoholic families about human willpower and its potential for good. Although self-help groups have a formal structure and organisation based upon the principles of the 12-step programme, they are not led by a professional or 'expert'.

You may remember that both Neil, the songwriter, and Jenny, the woman whose son attempted suicide, attended self-help groups as part of their recovery. Jenny went to Alcoholics Anonymous and Neil to Narcotics Anonymous.

Neil in particular was greatly helped. At his first NA meeting he was staggered by the reception he received. It mattered to people there that he was striving for recovery. They gave him their telephone numbers and taught him how to structure his day so as to give himself the best chance of sustained recovery. Most of all though, they showed him love, and their identification with him in his struggle against heroin reached him in a way that professional help could not. They had 'been there' themselves and they shared with him from their hearts the experiences of their own struggle with drugs. What made the greatest impression on Neil was that they told him they were sharing themselves with him because it was helping them to remain drug-free. They could only hang on to their own recovery so long as they shared it with others.

Six months after joining NA, Neil was giving away *his* telephone number to newcomers, and shortly before he finished his therapy with me he had given his first 'chair', in which he told his own story of addiction and recovery, one day at a time.

Al-Anon First and foremost of the self-help groups for children of alcoholics, this is the longest-standing and biggest self-help organisation for the families of alcoholics. There are many Al-Anon meetings each week throughout the UK. If you are presently living with an alcoholic and struggling with their drinking on a daily basis, then Al-Anon is by far the best contact for you.

In addition to the many ordinary Al-Anon meetings, this group has established two special subsidiaries: Al-Ateen, for teenagers from alcoholic families; and ACOA, for Adult Children of Alcoholics.

Adult Children of Alcoholics (ACA) is an independent self-help movement for adult children of alcoholics and other codependents, founded because the Al-Anon constitution seemed to some too restrictive. It is a very important source of help for adult children of alcoholics seeking to find recovery. I would recommend ACA as the first port of call for all adult children of alcoholics who are no longer living with an alcoholic parent.

Codependents Anonymous (CoDA)   is the newest self-help group for adult children of alcoholics and other codependents. It was formed because many codependents do not come from alcoholic backgrounds and they felt the need to have a group which did not specify alcoholics in its title. CoDA also emphasises recovery in the present, as opposed to emphasis on past events.

These self-help groups are described more fully in my previous book *Codependency*, which I wrote with Liz Hodgkinson in 1990. The resource section of this present book will give you direct access to them through their addresses and telephone numbers which you can use to find out more about them. My own view is that the differences between the groups are minimal as far as a newcomer to the self-help movement is concerned. You will be helped equally by contact with any one of them. In time, you will find the meetings and the style that best suits you. There are other self-help groups for adult children of alcoholics but I would suggest that you remain with one of those mentioned here for a while before venturing to try out any others.

Comforters   If we look at self-help groups in the context of the four role players then we can see that they are an excellent source of comfort. The only requirement for membership is that you have been affected by someone else's drinking. Members exchange telephone numbers and make themselves available to one another for support. In addition, there is a formal system of sponsorship in which the newcomer can choose a more experienced member of the group as a personal guide and mentor. An indication of the depth of support available within the self-help movement is the fact that many will make their self-help group their family of choice and find there a more fulfilling and reparative parenting than was possible in previous relationships.

Interpreters/translators   Self-help groups are an excellent source of this form of support. There is an abundance of information and an enormous accumulation of knowledge and experience, not only of the family disease of alcoholism but also of how to break free and live your own life.

Witnesses Self-help groups provide ample opportunity to find witnesses to what has happened to you and the lasting effects of your alcoholic upbringing. Most groups have a system of 'chairs' in which members in recovery take turns to tell their story to the group, including how their lives were affected by parental drinking, how they have faced up to their problems and what life in recovery is like for them. After some time in recovery, the new member will be asked to do a 'chair', and will thus have the chance to tell his/her own story.

Advocates Some self-help groups read a bill of rights at the beginning of each meeting, to emphasise the role of the self-help group as an advocate. The formation of a self-help group in itself is an act of advocacy, as adult children of alcoholics come out of hiding and begin the long task of understanding how they have been affected by parental alcoholism and the ways of breaking free which are available to them.

Professional help

There are various professional services available to adults and children who are suffering or have suffered distress. In the resource section there is information about organisations which I think offers good service and a couple of books detailing how to find a suitable professional helper.

The most likely source of professional help for adult children of alcoholics is a counsellor or psychotherapist. It is my view that professional help is best used only where:

• Your network of ordinary relationships cannot give you enough support.

- You are chronically stuck in your growth and development despite the best efforts of you and your support network.

- You choose for whatever reason to enhance the support and help already available to you.

- You find it impossible or undesirable to use self-help groups or other sources of help.

It is my experience that professional help will work better if you also attend a self-help group concurrently. The range of professional help available can be bewildering. A variety of professionals use the same title; for example, counsellor or 'psychotherapist', but practise in very different ways. Some basic distinctions can be made and you might find these helpful in choosing professional help. Remember that the terms psychotherapist or counsellor are not protected by law. In theory, anyone can set themselves up and make false claims. Make sure you approach a reputable professional body or organisation for assessment and referral.

In the resource section at the back of this book you will find names and addresses of groups who offer some safeguards. Although your local newspaper or yellow pages will print lists of professional helpers, and these people are probably *bona fide*, it is not worth the risk. At St Joseph's Centre, we assess clients from all over the UK and make referrals to local professionals. Although you would have to visit Haslemere for an assessment, this greatly reduces the risk of placing yourself in the hands of a bogus practitioner.

Psychotherapy Psychotherapists tend to undergo a more intensive training than counsellors. They train for longer periods, have intensive therapy themselves, and undergo rigorous scrutiny and supervision of their work while training. Psychotherapists are more likely also to have completed a previous professional training as a doctor, social worker, or psychologist. A course of psychotherapy lasts from a few months to a few years, according to the individual patient's needs.

Counselling Counsellors tend to be less highly trained but their training makes them better at working on specific problems in a time-limited and goal-oriented way. Counsellors tend to see clients for a period of months rather than years. If you are able to identify quite clearly the specific emotional or relationship problems from which you are suffering, then counselling support can be the best sort of help for you. If your questions about yourself are less well formed and the specific problems you identify are symptomatic of deeper ones, then treatment by a psychotherapist is more appropriate.

Counsellors tend to meet with clients on a once weekly basis, whereas psychotherapists prefer to see clients at least twice weekly, so that a more intensive relationship develops with the client and a fuller, deeper exploration of experience can take place.

Psychotherapy or counselling groups Some psychotherapists and counsellors undergo special training in group work. Typically, groups have between eight and 10 participants and a psychotherapist or counsellor as a facilitator or leader. Some clients prefer to be in a group because they can learn from others and find the group's support particularly beneficial. It also tends to be less costly than individual work.

Family therapy Practitioners of this form of therapy are hugely helpful in assisting the whole family to understand the rule system that governs their behaviour. They can help you and your family to understand the roles assigned to individual members, and how these roles can be relinquished so as to free up communication. Family therapists tend to organise between six and 12 sessions, on a fortnightly basis, with the family, or those family members who will attend.

Weekend workshops There are many weekend workshops and short experiential courses directed at people with various problems, including ACAs. These workshops can be very helpful, so long as you realise their limitations. If you need somewhere to go to 'let it all hang out' as it were, then they provide excellent value. If you are beginning to experiment with getting in touch with feelings, then weekend workshops can give a good experience. However, there is no substitute for ongoing and consistent support and help in dealing with codependency. Do not be misled into thinking that there are any quick fixes for your problems. This was a basic error in the thinking of your alcoholic family.

Fees

In some areas of the UK it is possible to have access to professional services of the sort outlined here on the NHS. In other areas NHS services are inadequate or non-existent. You are likely to have to pay for good professional help, although some institutions have low-cost help or reduced fees for those who cannot afford to pay the full amount.

Your first visit

The anticipation of a first visit to a professional can be very anxiety provoking, particularly if this is the first time you have ever asked for help.

An assessment interview can last for up to two hours. You will be asked why you are seeking help and what you see as the problems you are facing. You might also be asked to give a brief life history. The interviewer will be patient and listen carefully to your story. You might be asked to enlarge upon parts of it that are of particular relevance.

At the end of the interview, there will be time for you to ask questions about professional help and the interviewer will recommend a course of action. For example, s/he may refer you to a counsellor known to the interviewer and trusted to work to a professional standard. You will not have anything forced upon you and are free to decide whether you want to take up the recommended course of action, or not.

All *bona fide* professionals are bound by strict codes of

confidentiality and will not discuss your case, except with another professional who is similarly bound to confidentiality. Let us now see how such professionals rate, according to the four roles we have used previously.

Comforter   The professional has a limited role as comforter. S/he is unlikely to touch, hug, or hold you; ethics proscribe this behaviour for the professional. Some professionals argue that being understood in itself is tremendously comforting, because adult children of alcoholics have suffered greatly from a lack of thoughtful consideration from their parents, and that having a regular period of undivided attention from another human being is in itself comforting. My own view is that it is far more helpful for the professional to guide you towards your own internal and external comfort systems and to stay with you as you explore these than actively to be a comforter.

Interpreters/translators   Professionals can be vital sources of information and experience. They are likely to have studied child and adult development while training and to have learned how people can change ingrained patterns of behaviour. They will also have learned how to listen and to make some sense of your problems.

A potential drawback may occur if they do not recognise that alcoholism is a family disease and do not fully comprehend how a parent's drinking can so profoundly affect childhood development. The views on alcoholism and its effects offered by this book are not universally accepted. Codependence as a recognised phenomenon is very new, and many professionals are highly sceptical about what may appear to them to be the latest fad from America. Research and study on codependence is in its infancy and it is likely to be many years before acceptance of these ideas permeates medical and psychological wisdom.

This may or may not matter to ACAs seeking professional help. A good professional will always provide a structure within which you can explore your own thoughts and feelings and come to your own conclusions. S/he will provide the time and the space in which such exploration can take place, and make such exploration as safe as possible. It is a bonus if s/he understands alcoholism as a family disease and such knowledge will help you both.

However, there are some professionals who are not so skilled. Some may themselves be untreated ACAs, who will be very resistant to listening to your account of how parental alcoholism has affected you. You would be wise to avoid them. Although good training and professional accreditation is no guarantee of good treatment, it does build in safeguards.

Witness Professionals make excellent witnesses to your story. They are trained to be non-judgemental, good listeners. A competent professional is as good a witness as you are likely to find.

Advocate Professionals can be a good source of advocacy. Very quickly, they are likely to spot how low your self-esteem is and they will challenge statements you make which are self-deprecating or self-injurious. This will bring to the surface your negativity about yourself and make it harder for you to insult yourself or tolerate offensive comments from others. In such circumstances, many people will spontaneously draw up a bill of rights for themselves and allow others to become advocates on their behalf, or become better at self-advocacy and self-assertion.

Some professionals now base their professional role with clients on the premise of becoming advocates on behalf of the child within the adult client. Although I believe that, in some cases, such an approach can narrow the focus of therapy to an unacceptable degree, there is no doubting how effective such advocacy on behalf of the child within can be. It is particularly helpful to adult children of alcoholics because it emphasises the nurturing environment as the source of dysfunction in psychological development which, in turn, makes the professional very effective in supporting delayed childhood grieving over early losses.

Recovery as a personal quest

It is important to remember that whichever aids to recovery you choose to use, the most important person in your recovery is you. All the aids in the world are useless unless *you* are at the centre of your recovery and *you* are taking resonsibility for how it progresses.

CHAPTER 9

The Way Forward

IT's time now to stop looking backwards to our past or inward to our selves and the difficulties faced, and instead to look outwards at the key ways in which we can all, whether victims or helpers, work together towards a more enlightened, realistic, and positive attitude to alcoholism and its effects on family life.

Some of the groundwork has already taken place with the setting up of the National Association for Children of Alcoholics in the UK in 1989. The NACOA has four aims:

- To raise the profile of children of alcoholics in the public eye.

- To offer advice, information and fellowship to children of alcoholics.

- To educate and inform professionals.

- To promote research and study.

Why not send for information about the activities of NACOA and join us in our work for children of alcoholics? There is an enormous amount to be done by each of us in order to win a brighter future. In America, we have already been given a tremendous lead by the research there into children of alcoholics, through the National Association for Children of Alcoholics and the National Foundation for Children of Alcoholics in the USA. American professionals have provided a large literature on therapeutic approaches to codependency, and children of alcoholics in the USA have joined together in the self-help movement to aid each other in their struggles. Although we are not starting from scratch in the UK our base lines for information, advice, and research on children of alcoholics are at a low level and we must make massive strides foward in these areas.

Ending the stigma of alcoholism

First and foremost, we must tackle the stigmatism attached to alcoholism. Alcoholism *is* a disease. Alcoholics behave in the way they do because they are in the grip of a compulsion over which they are powerless. They do not observe their own compulsiveness in their drinking because their brains have become so pickled by alcohol that their capacity to link their drinking to the problems it causes is greatly diminished. Alcoholics in the grip of their addiction have become sick people, not bad or weak ones, and their whole selves are eventually given over to the service of the disease.

We would not punish a blind person because they can not see, yet we systematically punish alcoholics because they can not make the connection between their drinking and the destruction it wreaks on their body, mind and spirit. If the blind person falls over we pick them up and provide them with a white stick or a guide dog. When the alcoholic falls over we sneer, moralise – and turn away. We blame him for his fall and condone our behaviour by saying his problem is self-inflicted, therefore he is not worthy of help.

If we discovered a way of restoring sight to blind people, as a society we would be delighted. We would set up a major programme to inform blind people of the good news and get as many of them treated as possible, as quickly as finite resources would allow. Yet with the disease of alcoholism there is not the will at present to give alcoholics the chance to find recovery, despite the fact that we have treatment methods which would help at least half of all alcoholics and restore their health.

The treatment methods are not massively expensive but they do require that we begin from the premise that alcoholism is a treatable disease from which a full recovery is possible.

The medical and psychological establishment, currently under the sway of concepts such as harm minimisation and controlled drinking, would be well served by a renewed interest in the disease concept of alcoholism, and its usefulness as a therapeutic strategy. The present negative, narrow and ineffective perspectives on addiction held by the majority of clinicians in the UK fail not only the alcoholic but offer no hope or recognition to family members, especially children, whose suffering remains hidden and untreated.

As far as the general public is concerned, it is not difficult to understand why we moralise about alcoholism and attach stigma to it. The majority of us consume alcohol from time to time. We know our limit and stop drinking when we have had enough. When confronted by alcoholic drinking in another, we use the model of our own drinking pattern to make sense of what we see. We observe the excessive drinking and note that no one is forcing drinks down the alcoholic's throat. The alcoholic himself offers further evidence of the apparent wilfulness of his drinking by insisting that he could stop at any time and that he can 'hold' his liquor. When it becomes apparent that he can not, we react either by making a joke of it or by embarrassment and derision.

As I outlined in Chapter 1, alcoholics drink the way they do because their bodies react differently to alcohol. Whether this happens because they are born that way or because they acquire the disease through social interaction, or, as is more likely, a combination of the two, is irrelevant. The alcoholic's rationalisations and denial about his true relation to alcohol are attempts to hide his addiction from himself and others. Ordinary people unwittingly collude with the alcoholic's delusions because this accords with their own internal model of drinking based upon their own relationship to alcohol: that is, self-control is the solution to excessive drinking.

When we understand the disease concept of alcoholism it helps us to see the discrepancy between the utterances of the alcoholic about self-control and the reality of his powerlessness over his addiction. In so doing, it unburdens us of the anger, hatred, and vilification we sometimes direct towards the alcoholic. When we detach ourselves in this way we are freed from the need to moralise and condemn. We can love the alcoholic but hate what his illness does to him. We can hold him responsible for his recovery but not for having the disease in the first place. We can understand, too, the strains of this illness on family life and the dysfunction it creates. In such a context, children of alcoholics become visible and worthy of our time and attention.

A further block many of us have in facing up to alcoholism as a disease is that some alcoholics can seem like romantic rogues to us. We invite them to dinner parties to entertain our friends because when they have 'had a few' they have high entertainment value; can be charming, witty and outrageous, and can be relied upon to put on a performance. It seems to me that when we behave in this way we are carrying on a tradition which supposedly died out towards the end of the last century. In the Victorian era it was acceptable in our society to visit asylums and gain amusement from seeing the inmates. The 'freak shows' at the asylum involved displaying mentally or physically deformed people for our amusement.

It seems hard to imagine now that it could be acceptable for large numbers of people to enjoy such callous fun. Yet, I believe that if we look honestly at our use of the charming and amusing types of alcoholics at social functions, it becomes easy to understand our Victorian counterparts. We would all do well to re-evaluate our attitudes to excessive drinking and to any alcoholics we may number among our friends. When we stop laughing we may be appreciate the sadness of the spectacle and, perhaps, in years to come our grandchildren may find it incredible that in our generation the manifestations of the disease of alcoholism could have served such a cruel social function.

Advertising and the media

The present distorted perception of excessive drinking in our society is very heavily underpinned by images of alcohol promoted in the mass media. Although some advertisements for beer products are to be commended in recent years for their promotion of low- and no- alcohol beers, this is counterbalanced by the horrendous promotion of alcoholic drinking in others.

In the introduction to this book I mentioned the 'Carribbean island' escapism of drinking promoted in one advertisement. Another current advertising campaign extols the alcohol-centered attitude of the excessive drinker by declaring that Australians wouldn't give a XXXX for anything else. Yet another campaign associates the higher strength of high-alcohol beer with reinforced steel-like strength. The association is clear – strong beer, strong man.

So long as we continue to promote such images of excessive drinking we will continue to put at risk the most vulnerable in our society, our young people. Adolescents and young adults are very vulnerable to this type of advertising. They are very much concerned with image and identity, and alcohol advertising which connects with their desire to have a positive self-image is highly persuasive and dangerous.

Alcohol advertising should at least carry a clear warning that alcohol is an addictive drug, capable of causing harmful effects on health and wellbeing if not used with great caution. All alcohol products should carry information about recommended safe levels of consumption – 14 units per week for women and 21 units per week for men – and provide a telephone number to ring for further information, and counselling for those with drinking problems.

Distillers and brewers, surely, could collectively fund a helpline to provide information and advice for anyone worried about their own drinking or that of someone they know. Putting this information directly on alcohol products might bring it into the home of drinkers, where it would be visible to spouses and children of alcoholics. They might be willing to use the helpline, even if their drinking family member is not. The morning after the night before could be a different experience if, on clearing up the empty bottles, family members could find a telephone number on each bottle asking them to ring if they are worried about their own or someone else's drinking. They might just ring the number and become visible, and able to receive advice and help. If only children knew that they could not cause their parent to drink, could not control their parents drinking, and could not cure their parents drink problem, they might be considerably relieved. They are not alone in their struggles.

Labels on alcohol products, giving information about drinking problems, would also help to end the stigma attached to alcoholism by encouraging us all to talk about it and recognise it for what it is, a treatable illness.

Taxation policy

A very important and direct way of influencing the level of alcohol consumption is through the pricing of alcohol products. The more expensive alcohol becomes the less likely it is to be drunk in excess, particularly by teenagers and young adults. If they have £10 to spend on a Saturday evening they may see going to the pub and having 7 pints of lager as a reasonable return for their money. If they could buy only 3 pints for £10 then it might not seem like such a good deal. They might prefer to go to the cinema and have a hamburger afterwards. Young people going to the cinema and eating hamburgers are less likely to get into trouble afterwards than when they have consumed several pints of beer.

Pricing alcohol products at a high level would encourage thoughtful decisions to be made about the level of consumption. Sensible drinking would emerge from rational, thoughtful decisions about spending power rather than from any imperative about healthy or good behaviour. It is my view that young people are far more persuaded by spending power than the logic of healthy or good habits.

Older adults, too, may be persuaded to be more thoughtful about their alcohol consumption. Hardened drinkers, I am sure, would simply dig more deeply into their pockets and pay the extra money, and every alcoholic in the country would scream about the unfairness of vastly increasing the price of their addiction. However, we do know that alcoholics become able to face their addiction and its consequences when the price of continued drinking becomes too high. Increasing the financial cost of addiction would place an important pressure on the alcoholic to face up to his disease.

Higher taxation in the short term would lead to higher revenue returns, which could be earmarked to pay for addiction treatment services which at present are vastly underfunded. In the longer term, the savings to the National Health Service from reduced alcohol-related illness, and savings made on the police, probation, and prison services by the reduction in alcohol-related crime, would more than compensate for the reduction in revenue generated directly by alcohol taxation. The savings to industry from absenteeism from work would be an additional benefit. Of course, the savings to the family and its children in terms of human misery caused by excessive drinking would be immeasurable.

Ending the stigma attached to alcoholism by providing more information on alcohol products and tackling directly excessive drinking through a pricing policy would establish a solid platform from which to educate professionals and the general public about the effects of alcoholic drinking on the family and, in particular, the children.

Alcohol-related law breaking

Once we understand alcoholism as a disease it seems ridiculous to send alcohol-related offenders to prison. Instead, such offenders, need treatment and education. Drunk drivers, for instance, who are banned from driving could be required to demonstrate that they have received treatment for a drinking problem and achieved a period of abstinence before getting back their licence.

Violent offenders, who get into trouble after drinking, could have sentencing deferred for a year while they successfully complete a treatment course and demonstrate a trouble-free lifestyle.

This is not to advocate going soft on offenders. The alcoholic, like any other citizen, must be fully accountable for his actions, whether drunk or sober, but we can recognise that alcoholics act with diminished responsibility. As a society we can encourage them to understand their illness, and assist them in taking responsibility for their recovery and making a more positive contribution to society. Such an intervention, of course, must involve the family and give due recognition to the way they suffer from the family illness.

Children of alcoholics at school

In Appendix 1 on page 185 is a suggestion as to how children of alcoholics might be identified in the school setting, and how teachers might reach out to children and respond when they are approached for help. Schools have a vital role to play in the way forward for children of alcoholics. As we have seen, children of alcoholics appear in many guises. They might be quiet and withdrawn, or difficult and disruptive. They might also be high achievers, seeking recognition and affirmation through school performance.

Whichever way childhood codependence manifests itself, schools should have some idea how to respond to the needs of such children. At a very minimum, schools should recognise that such children exist and may have special educational needs. These are likely to vary from the need for remedial teaching to the need simply to have a little extra attention and encouragement. Children of alcoholics, although high achievers, may be lacking in social skills and a proper capacity to relate confidently to their peers or teachers. They may need encouragement to take part fully in the social activities of school life. They may be the child who inexplicably performs poorly under exam pressure, or is a poor attender, or who turns up late for school looking tired and hungry, or tearful.

Whichever manifestation presents itself, the teacher who is informed on the subject of family alcoholism can respond with understanding and sympathy.

Finally, let us all move forward to a full appreciation of the wonder of creation. We may become bruised, hurt, and damaged by our experiences but we can be restored. We have injured others in our fight for survival but we can be relieved of the burden of guilt. We were born as children of God, precious in His sight and full of the potential He wants us to fulfil. Our shame is conquered in His presence because His love is indefatigable. He is constantly moving in our direction. All that is required of us is that we respond with our hearts. Are you willing to respond? I did, in my own imperfect way, and continue as best I can, one day at a time. Your recovery and your liberation are at hand, just reach out with faith and patience – you will be found.

Postscript

IN THE course of this book I have shared with you details of psychotherapeutic work with three people, Neil, Jenny and Michael. Although the bulk of this book was written in the summer of 1991, I have the opportunity, while checking proofs in February 1992, to update you on their progress.

Neil has returned to his song writing career. Although he no longer sees me on a regular ongoing basis, as he has moved away from London, he has chosen to correspond with me every now and then. Our intensive work together may well be enough for him to get on with his life with all its ups and downs. He is able to be closer to his friends but still experiences considerable discomfort around intimate relationships. He remains free from all mood altering drugs and attends Narcotics Anonymous meetings on a regular basis. He attends ACA meetings on an irregular basis. It may be that Neil will resume his work with me for a further period in the future.

Jenny continues in her work with me. She has resumed face-to-face contact and has experienced no further relapse to alcohol use. Her general health and wellbeing have increased considerably. She reports feeling whole for the first time in her life. Her suicidal son has started going to ACA meetings. He has found the fellowship there to be of enormous benefit and his general attitude to life has changed dramatically for the better. It is highly unlikely that he will attempt suicide again. He has not needed any professional help. Her husband has stopped drinking and goes regularly to Alcoholics Anonymous meetings. He has not needed any professional help. Jenny has chosen not to use ACA or CoDA meetings.

Michael completed his work with me and our only correspondence since has been about gaining his permission to use his case material in this book. His therapy was a complete success. He is no longer controlled or pushed around by his dysfunctional past. He makes his own decisions and has gained peace of mind about his past. His greatest gain from psychotherapy was allowing his sense of humour to develop, and through this a wonderful connection was made with his children. His wife and he have had difficult times and were considering separation. These difficulties have been overcome and they now live in a closer relationship than ever was possible before. Michael did not find his attendance at self-help groups useful. It is unlikely that he will require any further professional help.

Appendix 1: A Guide for Schools: Children of Alcoholics in the Classroom

Teachers are ideally placed to detect and help the troubled children of alcoholics. Here are guidelines on what to look out for, and how to respond if you do spot such a child – or, indeed, the child spontaneously confides in you.

- A child fails to get excited about an anticipated class trip or event (because promises are so often broken at home).

- A child acts very differently during alcohol and drugs education from the way he or she usually reacts (for example, a talkative child becomes quiet, or a quiet child becomes animated).

- A child gets upset around his or her birthday and/or holidays (because special days are filled with disappointment for the child).

- A child wants time alone with a teacher or clings to a teacher or an aide (this represents an effort to get the nurturing he or she is not getting from a parent).

- A child has unrealistic expectations of other children and may be often disappointed in others (COAs often look to friends to provide the nurturing they are not getting at home).

- A child may not be able to comply with the requests of the school when these involve parents (for example, a student may not bring a permission slip, a smock, or an item from home for a project).

- A child may act out one of the adaptive roles COAs play in their families (see Chapter 4).

- A child is fearful of school-parent contact (because he or she fears that the parent will be drunk and the school will find out, or that the parent will behave inappropriately toward the teacher or abuse the child).

- A child talks back to a teacher or fights with another schoolchild (because he or she is angry at his or her parents, but can't express the anger and comes to school like a 'time bomb').

- A usually responsible child who does homework on time and does well on tests may inexplicably fail (for example, may offer no excuse or a far-fetched excuse for not having done homework or for doing poorly on a test – either of which may be covering up the real reason related to a parent's alcohol or drug use).

Of course, all children may present with one or more of these features on the odd occasion, and this does not mean they are necessarily children of alcoholics. But the appearance of some or many of these signs in a consistent way should alert the teacher that the child may well be the child of an alcoholic. So what can the teacher do?

Even without special training, a teacher can do much to aid children of alcoholics. The key to helping is to be able to recognise the nature of what the child is living with. Being able to listen is vital. Children of alcoholics are guarding a family secret that is struggling to come out. Being able to listen, understand and comfort will make a difference.

In time, you might be able to give the child some of the information you have learned about alcoholism. *Firstly*, alcoholism is a disease; alcoholics drink because they have a sickness, not because they are bad people or because they don't love their children. *Secondly*, nothing the child does or says causes a parent to drink, or to stop. All the child can reasonably do is to protect him/herself as best he or she can, perhaps by staying out of the way or even leaving the house if they feel threatened. *Thirdly*, the child is not alone; he or she is one of up to five million other such children in the UK. *Fourthly*, the child is a person of worth who deserves help. Tell them about Al-Ateen, the self help group for teenage children of alcoholics, if they are 13 or over. If they are younger, you may be the only source of outside support.

If you are a head teacher, or a member of a school governing body, perhaps you could introduce a policy to help children of alcoholics. You could consider the following points, suggested by the National Association for Children of Alcoholics in the USA, in any guidelines. As you will see, these have applications beyond the school setting and with minor alteration could be applied in any situation where adults are temporarily in charge of children.

- Do follow through if a child asks for help. You may be the only person the child has approached about the family problem. Courses of action you might choose are:

    Help the child contact a local Al-Ateen group, if they are 13 plus.

    Assist the child in 'thinking through' all of the sympathetic adults who play significant roles in his or her life (a favourite aunt or uncle, grandparent, scout leader, vicar or church person).

    Refer the child to an appropriate helping professional.

- Do develop and maintain a list of appropriate referrals. Knowing which organisations have resources to help children will make it easier when a child comes to you.

- Do maintain a small library of books and pamphlets, and reprints of articles on alcohol-related problems that have been written for children. Please enquire from the National Association for Children of Alcoholics in the UK what they might have available, or be aware of what is available elsewhere.

- Do be sensitive to possible cultural differences. If the child is from a different culture, it may be useful to explore that culture, including family structure, values, customs and beliefs. The cultural differences may influence how you can most effectively help the child.

- Don't behave in an embarrassed or uncomfortable way when the child asks you for help. Such a response may discourage the child and increase his or her sense of isolation and hopelessness.

- Don't criticise the child's parents or be overly sympathetic. The child may gain the greatest benefit just from having an adult friend with an understanding ear, who will advise where help can be found.

- Don't share the child's problems with others who do not have to know. This is not only important in terms of building trust with the child, but it also protects the child from being labelled by peers or other adults.

- Don't make plans with the child if you can't keep them. Stability and consistency in relationships are necessary if the child is to develop trust.

- Don't try to counsel the child unless you are trained to do so. Refer the child to someone with specialist skills, or help the child to contact a self-help group, if they are 13 plus.

Of course such policies are not introduced in a day, but even if such a proposal were offered for discussion by a governing body or at a weekly staff lunch/meeting, then it might be that the pieces begin to fall into place in understanding the behaviour of some members of the teacher's class.

Appendix 2: Notes

CHAPTER 1

1. Rowlands, in: *Hazardous Drinking*, Medical Council on Alcoholism, 1987.

2. Blum, et al, *Allelic Association of Human Dopamine D2 Receptor Gene in Alcoholism*, Journal of the American Medical Association, 263, 15, 2055 – 2060, April 1990.

3. Schuckit, M, *Twin Studies on Substance Abuse: An Overview*, in Gedda, Parisi and Nance, Eds, Twin Research 3. Epidemiological and Clinical Studies (New York: Alan R Liss, Inc., 1981).

4. Begleiter, H, *Event Related Brain Potentials in Boys at Risk for Alcoholism*, Science, 225, 1493 – 1496, 1984.

5. Schuckit, M, *Genetics and the Risk for Alcoholism*, Journal of the American Medical Association, 254, 18, pp. 2614 – 2617, November 1985.

6. Cermac, T, *Evaluating and Treating Adult Children of Alcoholics*, Vol 1 (Johnson Institute, 1990).

7. Birnbaum, I, *Study Links Women's Social Drinking with Sober-State Mood Disturbances*, Medical World News, Psychiatry Edition, p. 6, May 31st, 1984.

8. Levin, J, *Treatment of Alcoholism and Other Addictions: A Self Psychology Approach*, (Northvale, NJ: Jason Aronson, Inc., 1987).

9. Vaillant, G, *Adaptation to Life*, (Boston: Little, Brown & Co, 1977).

10. Coates, M, & Paech, G, *Alcohol and Your Patient: A Nurses' Handbook*, Canada: Addiction Research Foundation, 1979.

11. Ackerman, R, *Children of Alcoholics: A Guide for Parents, Educators and Therapists* (New York, Simon & Schuster, 1983).

12. Reddy, B, *Alcoholism, A Family Illness*, Park Ridge, Illinois: Lutheran General Hospital, 1983.

13. Brooks, B, *The Secret Everyone Knows*, Operation Cork, 1981.

CHAPTER 2

1. Schneiderman, I, *Family Thinking in Prevention of Alcoholism*, Preventive Medicine, 4, pp. 296–309, 1975.

2. Moos, R. & Billings, A, *Children of Alcoholics during the Recovery Process; alcoholic and matched control families*, Addictive Behaviours, 7, pp. 155–163, 1982.

3. Nylander, I, *Children of Alcoholic Fathers* (Acta Paedidiatrica, 49, Suppl. 121(1), 1960).

4. Putnam, S, *Are Children of Alcoholics Sicker than Other Children? A Study of Illness Experience and Utilisation Behavior in a Health Maintenance Organisation*, Paper presented to American Public Health Association, November 1985.

5. Matajcek, Z, & Baueriva, N, *Health Status of Children from Alcoholic Families*, Csekoslovenska Pediatrie, 36, pp. 588–592, 1981.

6. Marcus, A, *Academic Achievement in Elementary School Children of Alcoholic Mothers*, Journal of Clinical Psychology, 42, pp. 372–376, 1986.

7. Ervin, C, et al, *Alcoholic Fathering and its Relation to Child's Intellectual Development: A Pilot Investigation*, Alcoholism:

Clinical and Experimental Research, 8, pp. 362 – 365, 1984.

8. Fine, E, et al, *Behavioral Disorders in Children with Parental Alcoholism*, Annals New York Academy of Sciences, 273, pp. 507 – 517, 1976.

9. Herjanic, B, et al, *Children of Alcoholics*, in: Seixas, F, *Currents in Alcoholism* (New York, Grunne & Stratton)

10. Miller, D, and Jang, M, *Children of Alcoholics: A 20-Year Longitudinal Study*, Social Work Research, 13, pp. 23 – 29, 1979.

11. Erikson, Erik, *Childhood and Society*, (New York: W W Norton & Co, 1963).

12. Barnes, J, et al, *Psychosocial Characteristics of Women with Alcoholic Fathers* in: M, Galanter, *Currents in Alcoholism, Treatment, and Rehabilitation and Epidemiology* (New York, Grune & Stratton).

13. Pyle, R, et al, *Bulimia: A Report of 34 Cases*, Journal of Clinical Psychiatry, 42, pp. 60 – 64, 1981.

14. Johnson, S, et al, *Children of Alcoholics, Drinking Styles and Drug Use*, Paper presented at the Research Society on Alcoholism (San Fransisco, CA, 1986).

15. Tishler, C, & McKenry, P, *Parental Negative Self and Adolescent Suicide Attempts*, Journal of the American Academy of Child Psychiatry, 21, pp. 404 – 408, 1982.

16. Lawson, G, et al, *Alcoholism and The Family*, Rockville, MD, Aspen System Corp, 1983.

17. Werner, E, *Resilient Offspring of Alcoholics: A Longitudinal Study from Birth to Age 18*, Journal of Studies on Alcohol, 47, pp. 34 – 40 1986.

CHAPTER 3

1. Black, Claudia, *It Will Never Happen To Me* (New York: Ballentine, 1987).

2. Wegscheider-Cruse, Sharon, *Another Chance: Hope and Health for the Alcoholic Family* (Palo Alto, CA: Science and Behaviour Books, 1981).

3. Bradshaw, J, *Bradshaw on the Family* (Health Communication, Inc., 1989).

4. Bowlby, J, *Attachment and Loss, Volume 2: Separation: Anxiety and Anger* (New York, Basic Books, 1973).

5. Moorhouse, E, & Tarpley, R, *An Examination of Dysfunctional Latency Age Children of Alcoholic Parents and Problems in Intervention*, in: Ackerman, R, *Growing in the Shadow*, Health Communications, Inc., 1986.

CHAPTER 4

1. Woititz, J, *Adult Children of Alcoholics*, Health Communications, Inc., 1983.

CHAPTER 7

1. Cermac, Timmen, *A Primer on Adult Children of Alcoholics*, (Pompano Beach, Fl: Health Communications, Inc., 1985).

2. Cermac, Timmen, *A Time to Heal* (Los Angeles: Jeremy P. Tarcher, Inc., 1988).

3. Woititz, J, *Healing Your Sexual Self*, Health Communications, Inc., 1989.

4. *Alcoholics Anonymous, The Big Book*, Hazell, Watson, & Viney Ltd, 1976.

CHAPTER 8

1. Baker, A, & Duncan, S, *A Psychological Model of Codependency*, Paper presented to National Association for Children of Alcoholics Conference, Haslemere, Surrey, May 1990.

Appendix 3: Further Reading

ADULT CHILDREN OF ALCOHOLICS

Adult Children of Alcoholics, Janet Woititz, Health Communications, Inc.
ACOA Syndrome, Wayne Kritzberg, Health Communications, Inc.
A Time to Heal, Timmen Cermac, Avon Books.
Grandchildren of Alcoholics, Ann Smith, Health Communications, Inc.
Healing the child Within, Charles Whitfield, Health Communications, Inc.

ADDICTION

Painful Affairs: Looking for Love through Addiction and Codependency, Joseph R Cruse, Health Communications, Inc.
The Thirsty Muse, Tom Dardis, Abacus Books.
Women, Sex and Addiction, Charlotte Davis Kasl, Mandarin Books.

CODEPENDENCY

Choicemaking, Sharon Wegscheider Cruse, Health Communications, Inc.
Codependency, David Stafford and Liz Hodgkinson, Piatkus Books.
Codependent No More, Melody Beattie, Hazelden.
Codependents' Guide to the Twelve Steps, Melody Beattie, Piatkus Books.
Facing Codependency, Pia Melody, Harper Row.
Homecoming, John Bradshaw, Piatkus Books.

SPIRITUAL PATH

Jonathan Livingston Seagull, Richard Bach, Pan Books.
God of Surprises, Gerald Hughes, Darton, Longman & Todd.
Ordering Your Private World, Gordon MacDonald, Highland Books.
The Prophet, Kahil Gibran, Pan Books
The Road Less Travelled, Scott Peck, Arrow Books

COUNSELLING and PSYCHOTHERAPY
Counselling, Liz Hodgkinson, Simon & Schuster.
The Counselling Handbook, Susan Quilliam, Thorsons.
Counselling and Psychotherapy, Is it for me?, Hetty Einzig, British Association for Counselling (see Appendix 4).
Counselling and Psychotherapy Resource Directory, British Association for Counselling.

GENERAL

The Drama of Being a Child Alice Miller, Virago Books.
The Innocence of Dreams, Charles Rycroft, Chatto and Windus.
For Your Own Good, Alice Miller, Virago Books.
My Mother My Self, Nancy Friday, Fontana Books.
My Secret Garden, Nancy Friday, Quartet Books.
The Tyranny of Malice, Joseph Berke, Simon & Schuster.

Most of these books should be available from major bookshops. If you experience difficulty, please contact:

Compendium Books, 234 Camden High Street,
London NW1
071-267 1525

Watkins, 19-21 Cecil Court, London WC2N 4EZ
071-836 2182

Quest Books, River House, 46 Lea Road, Waltham Abbey,
Essex EN9 1AJ
0992 88771

Appendix 4: Useful Addresses

SELF-HELP GROUPS

The following self-help groups have national offices which can be contacted for information about local groups in your area.

Alcoholics Anonymous
PO Box 1
Stonebow House
Stonebow
York
YO1 2NJ
Tel: 0904 644026

London Service Office
Tel: 071-352-3001

AA offers support and information to problem drinkers. The only criterion for using an AA group is that you are a problem drinker with a desire to stop drinking.

Narcotics Anonymous
PO Box 704
London SW10 0RP
Tel: 071-351 6794 or 071-351 6066

NA offers support and information to problem illicit or pre-scribed drug users. The only criterion for using an NA group is that you are a problem drug user with a desire to stop.

Al-Anon Family Groups
61 Great Dover Street
London SE1 4YF
Tel: 071-403 0888

Al-Anon offers support and information to family members or friends of problem drinkers. The only criterion for using an Al-Anon group is that your life brings you into contact with a problem drinker. Al-Ateen is a special group for teenagers where a parent is a problem drinker. ACOA is a special group for adult children of alcoholics.

Families Anonymous
650 Holloway Road
London N19 3NU
Tel: 071-281 8889

FA offers advice and information to family members or friends of problem drug takers. The only criterion for using an FA group is that your life brings you into contact with a problem drug taker.

Codependents Anonymous
PO Box 1292
London N4 2XX
Tel: 071-409 0029

CoDA is for anyone who recognises a problem of codependency and is seeking to grow from it.

Adult Children of Alcoholics
The Information Officer
33 Upper Whistler Walk
London SW10 0ER
Tel: Frances, 071-376 5205

ACA is for anyone who recognises the impact of growing up in a family with a parent who is alcoholic, or for those who can identify similar dysfunctional patterns in their family of origin, and wish to grow from them. Anyone who is codependent for whatever reason can use ACOA or ACA.

GENERAL INFORMATION AND ADVICE

The British Association for Counselling
1 Regents Place
Rugby
Warwickshire CV21 2PJ
Tel: 0788 578328

The BAC gives accreditation to individual counsellors and approves good counsellor training programmes. They produce information for those seeking a counsellor and a listing of trained and qualified counsellors throughout the UK.

The National Association for Children of Alcoholics
PO Box 64
Fishponds
Bristol BS16 2UE
Tel: 0800 289 0611 or 0272 573432

NACOA is a charity which has four broad aims: raising the profile of children of alcholics (COAs) in the public consciousness; reaching professionals who deal with COAs in their everyday work and educating them as to the needs of COAs; offering advice, information, and fellowship to COAs; promoting research into the phenomenon of COAs.

PROFESSIONAL SERVICES

St Joseph's Centre for Addiction
Holy Cross Hospital
Hindhead Road
Haslemere
Surrey
GU27 1NQ
Tel: 0428 656517

St Joseph's offers a comprehensive range of services to drug and alcohol dependent people and their families, including detoxification and in-patient rehabilitation. The Codependency Clinic is an out-patient service offering help to codependent people whether or not drugs or alcohol are involved.

The Chemical Dependency Centre
11 Redcliffe Gardens
London SW10 9BG
Tel: 071-352 2552

CDC run an out-patient clinic offering assessment, diagnosis and referral, individual counselling, group therapy, and after-care, for chemically dependent people. Services are provided regardless of whether patients can pay for them or not.

Arbours Consultation Service
6 Church Lane
London N8 7BU
Tel: 081-340 7646 or 081-348 6466

The Arbours Consultation Service offers assessment for psychotherapy and referral to trained and experienced psychotherapists. There is a low-cost psychotherapy service where patients are seen by student psychotherapists under supervision from experienced psychotherapists. This service *is not suitable for those who are chemically dependent*.

Westminster Pastoral Foundation
23 Kensington Square
London W8 5HN
Tel: 071-937 6956

WPF offers an excellent counselling service to a wide range of people with various problems. It also has associated coun-selling services in many parts of the country. WPF trained counsellors tend to be of a high quality. This service *is not suitable for those who are chemically dependent*.

Institute for Self-Analysis
12 Nassington Road
London NW3 2UD
Tel: 071-794 4306

The ISA bases its novel form of psychotherapy around the idea of advocacy on behalf of the child within. It draws its inspiration from the work of Alice Miller, Karin Horney and John Bowlby. Many children of alcoholics find their approach to psychotherapy helpful. This service is not suitable for those who are chemically dependent.

Rape Crisis Centre
PO Box 69
London WC1X 9NJ
Tel: 071-837 1600 or 071-278 3956

The Rape Crisis Centre has a 24-hour answering service. They will help women who have been raped recently or in the past. They are particularly helpful to those who were sexually abused as children.

Women's Therapy Centre
629 Manor Gardens
London N7 6LA
Tel: 071-263 6200

The WTC offers advice and information to women with all sorts of difficulties and problems. The psychotherapy service offered is particularly good for those with eating disorders and/or sexual issues.

Ashwood Centre
Ashwood Road
Woking
Surrey GU22 7JR
Tel: 0483 747685

The Ashwood Centre hosts a team of child care consultants. The core of their clerical work is with children and young people affected by trauma of various sorts. They are particularly good with adults who suffered childhood trauma and have facilities for treating whole families. The Centre is suitable for use by those who are chemically dependent and their families.

Index

Piatkus Books

If you are interested in recovery, health and personal growth, you may like to read other titles published by Piatkus.

RECOVERY

Adult Children of Divorce: *How to achieve happier relationships* Dr Edward W Beal and Gloria Hochman (Foreword by Zelda West-Meads of *RELATE*)

At My Father's Wedding: *Reclaiming our true masculinity* John Lee

Children of Alcoholics: *How a parent's drinking can affect your life* David Stafford

The Chosen Child Syndrome: *What to do when a parent's love rules your life* Dr Patricia Love and Jo Robinson

Codependents' Guide to the Twelve Steps: *How to understand and follow a recovery programme* Melody Beattie

Codependency: *How to break free and live your own life* David Stafford and Liz Hodgkinson

Don't Call it Love: *Recovery from sexual addiction* Dr Patrick Carnes

Homecoming: *Reclaiming and championing your inner child* John Bradshaw

Obsessive Love: *How to free your emotions and live again* Liz Hodgkinson

HEALTH

Acupressure: *How to cure common ailments the natural way* Michael Reed Gach

The Alexander Technique: *How it can help you* Liz Hodgkinson

Aromatherapy: *The encyclopedia of plants and oils and how they can help you* Danièle Ryman

Arthritis Relief at Your Fingertips: *How to use acupressure massage to ease your aches and pains* Michael Reed Gach

The Enclopedia of Alternative Health Care: *The guide to choices in healing* Kristin Olsen

Herbal Remedies: *The complete guide to natural healing* Jill Nice

Hypnosis Regression Therapy: *How reliving early experiences can improve your life* Ursula Markham

Increase Your Energy: *Regain your zest for life the natural way*
Louis Proto

Infertility: *Modern treatments and the issues they raise*   Maggie Jones

Nervous Breakdown: *What is it? What causes it? Who will help?*   Jenny Cozens

The Reflexology Handbook: *A complete guide*
Laura Norman and Thomas Cowan

Self-Healing: *How to use your mind to heal your body*
Louis Proto

The Shiatsu Workbook: *A beginners' guide*   Nigel Dawes

Spiritual Healing: *All you need to know*   Liz Hodgkinson

Super Health: *How to control your body's natural defences*
Christian H Godefroy

Super Massage: *Simple techniques for instant relaxation*
Gordon Inkeles

Women's Cancers: *The treatment options*   Donna Dawson

PERSONAL GROWTH

Colour Your Life: *Discover your true personality through colour*
Howard and Dorothy Sun

Dare to Connect: *How to create confidence, trust and loving relationships*   Susan Jeffers

Fire in the Belly: *On being a man*   Sam Keen

Living Magically: *A new vision of reality*   Gill Edwards

The Passion Paradox: *What to do when one person loves more than the other*   Dr Dean C Delis with Cassandra Phillips

Protect Yourself: *How to be safe on the streets, in the home, at work, when travelling*   Jessica Davies

The Power of Gems and Crystals: *How they can transform your life*   Soozi Holbeche

The Right to be Yourself: *How to be assertive and make changes in your life*   Tobe Aleksander

For a free brochure with further information on our range of titles, please write to:

Piatkus Books,
Freepost 7 (WD 4505),
London W1E 4EZ

CODEPENDENCY
by David Stafford and Liz Hodgkinson

Codependents are people who have to depend on others for their own sense of self-worth and self-esteem. Although the term is relatively new, the syndrome is extremely common. With the use of case histories, this book shows:

- How codependency starts
- How it manifests itself
- How the problems it causes can be overcome

By reading this much-needed book you will come to recognise and understand the codependency syndrome and learn how to break free from it and live your own life. David Stafford is a psychoanalytic psychotherapist and Director of the St Joseph's Centre for Addiction at Holy Cross Hospital, Haslemere, Surrey, which specialises in codependency. Liz Hodgkinson is a medical writer.

CODEPENDENTS' GUIDE TO THE TWELVE STEPS
by Melody Beattie

Millions of people around the world identified with Melody Beattie in *Codependent No More* and gained inspiration from her in *Beyond Codependency*. In her new book she helps you to discover how recovery programmes work and shows you how to interpret the famous Alcoholics Anonymous Twelve Steps specially for codependent issues. *Codependents' Guides to the Twelve Steps* will show you how to:

- Understand each step, and discover how you can apply it to your life
- Use specific exercises and activities both in group settings and on your own
- Find out more about the wide range of Twelve Step programmes
- Follow a recovery programme

In her uniquely warm and compassionate way, Melody Beattie will inspire you to turn your life around − one step at a time.

ADULT CHILDREN OF DIVORCE
by Dr Edward W Beal and Gloria Hochman

Adult Children of Divorce speaks directly to the millions of people who are still recovering from seeing their homes torn apart. Based on years of research and over 300 case histories, it answers the critical questions:

● What happens to a child of divorce when he or she becomes an adult and tries to form relationships, get married and have children?
● How do the ghosts of the failed marriage in the past return?
● How can adult children of divorce break the cycle, before it's too late?

This is an enormously helpful book for the many people still handicapped by a broken past. Dr Edward Beal is a practising psychiatrist and associate professor of psychiatry at Georgetown University Medical Centre. Gloria Hochman is a writer specialising in medicine, psychology and social welfare.

DON'T CALL IT LOVE
by Dr Patrick Carnes

● 'I lost three marriages, all because of affairs.'
● 'I went to porn films during work time, although I did not want to.'
● 'I spent money on sex when I needed it for children's clothes.'

For some men and women sex is like a drug they cannot do without. *Don't Call it Love* is based on 1,000 interviews with sex-addicted people and their families. It looks at sex addiction in all its various aspects and shows you how to get help and start to rebuild your life and reclaim a healthy sexuality.

Dr Patrick Carnes is the world's foremost expert on sexual addiction, and the author of several important books in the field of sexual health.

HOMECOMING: RECLAIMING AND CHAMPIONING YOUR INNER CHILD
by John Bradshaw

John Bradshaw is a major figure in the field of recovery and dysfunctional families. His 'inner child' work is a powerful, new therapeutic tool. The people who come to his workshops bring with them persistent problems such as addiction, depression, troubled relationships and chronic dissatisfaction. He helps them to reach back to the source of their problems – their childhood and adolescence – and understand how the wounds received then can continue to contaminate their adult lives. He offers them the chance to reclaim and nurture their 'inner child' and grow up again. This experience has transformed their lives. Reading this book will help you to transform your life and find a new joy and energy in living.

THE CHOSEN CHILD SYNDROME
by Dr Patricia Love and Jo Robinson

The Chosen Child Syndrome addresses a problem of major importance in the lives of millions of men and women. It looks at what can happen when a parent depends on a child – rather than a spouse or adult friend – for emotional and psychological support. Were you a chosen child?

- Was one of your parents your best friend?
- Were you the source of emotional support for your mother or father?
- Did your mother or father have unrealistic expectations of you?
- Did you sometimes feel invaded by your mother or father?
- Were potential boyfriends or girlfriends never 'good enough'?

Dr Patricia Love is a marriage and family therapist. In *The Chosen Child Syndrome* she offers a recovery programme which will help all family members. It will also help chosen children to create a loving, balanced relationship with their parents – and their own children.

AT MY FATHER'S WEDDING
by John Lee

At My Father's Wedding is a powerful, moving and compassionate book which examines why contemporary men find it hard to get in touch with their feelings, and why they find it difficult to commit, to give, to receive or to express themselves emotionally. In this book, John Lee offers men a way to improve the quality of their lives and their relationships with men and women. It looks at the negative messages that men give themselves and examines why the majority of men are so remote from their feelings. Written in a poetic and deeply personal style, John Lee − a major writer on men's issues − helps men to explore their relationship with their fathers, take down the defensive walls they have built around themselves, and feel good about being a man.

DARE TO CONNECT
by Susan Jeffers

Dare to Connect is for everyone who has ever asked:
- Why do I feel so nervous when I walk into a room full of strangers?
- Why do I feel lonely, even though I'm surrounded by people?
- Why do I feel so alienated from my husband/wife/lover?
- How can I pick up the phone and make that important call without feeling anxious?

We all want to be liked or loved and to feel close to our partners, friends and colleagues. What we don't always know is how to make the connection. In this empowering book, Susan Jeffers gives us the insights and tools we need to end our loneliness and create a sense of belonging everywhere we go. Susan Jeffers has a doctorate in psychology and is a noted public speaker and workshop leader. Her books on fear, relationships and personal growth have been international bestsellers.